Tempus ORAL HISTORY *Series*

Please return or renew this item by the last date shown.
You may renew items (unless they have been requested
by another customer) by telephoning, writing to or calling
in at any library.   100% recycled paper   *BKS 1 (5/95)*

The main road from Oundle to Peterborough outside Tansor Lodge Farm when the Preston family lived there. It is hard to realise it is the busy A 605 today.

Tempus ORAL HISTORY *Series*

voices of
the Nene Valley

Compiled by
Judith Spelman

TEMPUS

First published 2001
Copyright © Judith Spelman, 2001

Tempus Publishing Limited
The Mill, Brimscombe Port,
Stroud, Gloucestershire, GL5 2QG

ISBN 0 7524 2441 6

Typesetting and origination by
Tempus Publishing Limited
Printed in Great Britain by
Midway Colour Print, Wiltshire

Dedication

For Mary Thomson, *née* Howard, whose memories of living along the edge of the Nene Valley
as a girl remain so vivid.

Acknowledgements

My thanks go especially to His Royal Highness the Duke of Gloucester for kindly providing the
Foreword to the book.

I am indebted also to all those wonderful people who have given their time to share their
memories with me; to those who have loaned me photographs – especially Reg Sutton MBE
and Norah Blunt, who both allowed me to ransack their substantial collections – to Juliet Wilson
who talked to me about the different names of the river, and to the many people who have
offered suggestions, contacts and advice. I am also very grateful to Nigel Simmance for giving
me technical support.

Contents

Foreword

It has been famously said that 'the past is like a foreign country'. As the rate of change increases, so each generation surprises both the next and the previous.

Judith Spelman has explored this 'foreign country', inviting people in the Nene Valley to reminisce on the past and the ways of previous generations. And so familiar names, buildings and landscapes surprise us with old problems and concerns which no longer worry us – the great amount of time spent on mundane things we do in seconds.

I recall as a small child going out to see my father helping gather in the hay harvest, armed with a pitchfork, on a hot summer's day. 'Why, Papa, are you all wet when it has not been raining?' Sadly, I cannot recall his reply, which was probably much riper and more memorable than the question!

It is difficult to imagine days of farming before mechanization. I recall taking a Nigerian visitor to watch the harvest coming in with combine harvesters and tractors and trailers, to bring the corn home. 'In my country it would take one hundred people to achieve this.' Today we have even bigger machines and fewer people to achieve the same output.

I remember that in one of our larger fields a few years ago they were still combining one end of the field, ploughing and cultivating in the middle and drilling rape at the far end. There were no less than fifteen machines in one field. Today, we could not manage more than five or six but we grow as much. Barnwell used to be considered a big farm; today, although the same size, it is considered by some 'marginal' to 'too small' for the true economies of scale.

It is not surprising that I can remember the splendid puffing noises of the steam trains going from Barnwell to Oundle back in the 1950s, but also cows being milked by hand, when the dairy was in the stable yard at the Manor. I got into big trouble for persuading the milkman to take me in his motorcycle and sidecar down to the village – no doubt to call on Mrs Pask in the village shop.

Lady Ethel Wickham, mentioned by Ann Cheney **(page?)** as one of Mr Amps' customers, used to live at Barnwell Manor until my Grandfather sold it in the 1900s and she moved to Tansor. I remember she came to visit when Queen Mary was staying; they remembered meeting at Ascot in 1888 and they recalled the event with amazing clarity because it was an important social event for two teenage girls! Lady Ethel was personally a monument to the extension of generations. Her father had fought in the Battle of Waterloo (aged eighteen) and her grandfather had danced with Marie Antoinette. Both of them produced their offspring in extreme old age!

The author has compiled similar books for other communities and her skill lies in finding the right people to recall how different the experience of previous generations is to our own and how they fitted in to the order of the day. I hope *Voices of the Nene Valley* will encourage older readers, surprise younger ones and will entertain and intrigue us all.

HRH Duke of Gloucester, KG GCVO

The Duke of Gloucester taking part in a tug o' war at Castle Farm, Barnwell as part of the Queen's Silver Jubilee celebrations.

Introduction

It is a privilege to talk to so many people whose memories vividly span many decades. Some people I have known for years, some I met for the first time, but they all had stories to tell that are fascinating and give a glimpse of life in the first half of the twentieth century.

I cannot vouch for accuracy because memory can be extraordinarily fickle and very occasionally you may find contradictions. When that happens, you can make up your own mind! The importance of this book lies in the personal experiences of the people; all major events are documented over the years but how people lived through them has only in recent years been recognised as important. Libraries and museums throughout the country are recording memories to make a bank of oral history that will complement factual data. Once people die, their memories die with them.

This book is called *Voices of the Nene Valley* because the river in some way, deliberately, accidentally or remotely, touches the lives of people living near by. In it are the memories of people living between Peterborough and Northampton, the majority close to the market towns of Thrapston and Oundle.

In compiling this book, I have learnt how to make a feather mattress from chicken, duck and goose feathers, clean a house properly, butcher a pig and make hock'n dough for dinner. I marvel at the miles adults and children walked and cycled, at the efficient railway system with stations serving most of the villages and the strong sense of community. It is interesting that most of these memories are happy ones.

Donald Akroyd, a solicitor and retired clerk to the Nene River Board, talked to me about the river. It is a good coarse fishing river for bream, carp, rudd and tench, a fact that many angling clubs will ascertain. The National Federation of Anglers hold their competitions locally from time to time, when there is concentrated fishing along the river from The Dog in a Doublet beyond Peterborough right up to Wansford.

The Nene River Board was established in 1952, succeeding the Nene Catchment Board that was set up in 1930 and was concerned mainly with land drainage. The River Board functioned until 1965 when it became The Welland & Nene River Authority responsible for land drainage, pollution and fisheries as well as taking on a new, important responsibility for water resources that in due course led to creating Rutland Water.

Then there is the name of the river, or more correctly the pronunciation of the name. It changes, I am reliably informed, somewhere between Oundle and Thrapston, probably in the Barnwell area. From there to Northampton the river is pronounced Nen; in the opposite direction through Oundle and away to Peterborough and the sea, it is pronounced Nene. Both pronunciations are adhered to strongly by local residents. Get it wrong at your peril!

There is the suggestion, according to Donald Akroyd, that there were nine sources of the river Nene, which could be the origin of its name. It has been referred to over the years as Nine, Nyn and Nyne, Nynne, Ninne, Neen, Nynfluve, Avon, Nien, Nenna, Ene, Nenn and Antona. Some early Acts of Parliament, passed at a time when it was considered practical to make the river navigable, refer to the river as 'Nen alias Nine'.

The more accepted number, offered by Cheryl Joyce, Nene Valley Access Officer, is that there are three sources of the river, all in Northamptonshire; one rises a mile west of Badby, another near Arbury Hill and a third at Yelvertoft.

Thames barges were coming up the river to Peterborough and Cadge & Colman's on a regular basis until the late 1960s. Narrow barges came from the Grand Union Canal and down the Nene to Wellingborough. But the railways that were opened in the mid-1800s took the trade.

The Nene was in a parlous state as far as land drainage was concerned until the catchment board came into operation in 1931, explains Donald Akroyd. Then the locks (there are twenty-seven between Northampton and Peterborough) were all rebuilt in an effort to encourage more use of the river. There was even the possibility of an inland port at Peterborough and a bridge, the Fitzwilliam Bridge, was built across the river in order to provide access to it.

Many local people, such as John Jeffs of Islip and Bert Hastings of Barnwell, worked on the river. In the 1930s it was all manual labour and the River Board had a foreman living in every third or fourth village along the river. When there was a flood alert, a telephone call would go from man to man and they would get on their bikes, day or night, and cycle over to check the river levels.

Over the years the river has flooded regularly causing not only damage but also a fair amount of ingenuity among the local population. Jack Starsmore was not deterred from delivering milk;

he used a punt to take him to homes in Yarwell and Nassington, on the way ferrying people across the water to the station platorm. According to Donald Akroyd the flood of all time was in 1947, but only three years ago the Easter floods caused havoc all along the valley. He recalls ringing the coal merchants at Thrapston who told him their coal lorries in Midland Road were under water and apparently had several feet of water in the offices.

When I moved to the area in the 1970s, I was anxious to discover more about it but there were no local books to tell me. Now there are many excellent ones and I hope *Voices of the Nene Valley* will be an interesting and useful addition.

Judith Spelman
August 2001

The first Thrapston Girl Guides in 1946 with their captain, Miss C.W. MacQueen (centre left)

CHAPTER 1

Early Memories

Norah Marriott, aged 10.

A Garage in Thrapston

My mother's name was Betty Carress. Her parents had a garage in Thrapston called Heightons, which was in the market place. When I was a child we used to go over there and I used to stay with my father's mother. We loved to go down to the garage and during the war my grandfather, Jack Carress, was to do with the war agricultural committee and he used to take me with him when he was visiting the farms in the area. He died in 1947.

Ann Cheney

Family History

The Prestons were a Tansor family that went back well into the 1700s. I was born at Tansor Lodge cottage in the bedroom that looks out onto the road. My grandfather, Philip Preston, came to Tansor Lodge in 1908 after he married. My father, Ted Preston, joined him on the farm when he left school and my uncle, Tim (his name was really Harold) joined him later on. So I lived at Tansor Lodge Cottage all my life until I sold it in 1995 to Mrs Anne Brown.

John Preston

A Farming Family

I was born at Home Farm in Great Addington. My father was Bert Howard and he was born in the village of Holme just outside Peterborough. Father used to play the organ at Hemington church and mother was part of the congregation and that is how they met. My father went on to be a pupil-farmer with my mother's eldest brother – she had seven. His name was John Lawrence and he farmed at Marston just outside Bedford and father was there for five years. When he came back they bought the farm at Great Addington about 1910. He was sixty-four when he died. My mother left the farm eventually and moved into Oundle.

Mary Thomson

By Pony and Buggy

I was called Winnie all my life but I am really Florence and I prefer to be called that. I was born in Brakehill Farm in Lower Brigstock park. My memories go back to 1910 when I was five years old. I remember going to school in a pony and buggy with my younger sister. My father had three ponies and used to take the milk and deliver it to an uncle who would then take it around Peterborough. Another of my uncles would deliver milk around Kettering. I had another uncle who had a bakehouse on the corner of King Street in Kettering.

Florence Gray

Stir that Pudding

When I was ten or twelve I had to help deliver the milk. We would go in the back door and fill up a jug that was left out for us.

'Tim' Harold Preston at Tansor Lodge Farm in the late 1920s.

I remember one lady one day coming down the road and I was a bit late. She told me when I got to her house to put half the milk in the rice pudding and give it a stir.

Jack Starsmore

Three Partners

I was born in Northampton but we were living at Queen Anne's in West Street, Oundle, where the doctor's surgery was, and next to the Stahl Theatre. We lived on the top floor and the surgery was on the bottom floor. At that time the Stahl Theatre was the Congregational Church. My father was Ivor Spurrell. He came to Oundle and joined his uncle, Bernard Turner, who lived at 22 Benefield Road. Another of the partners was a Doctor Elliott and he lived on the corner of North Street just before you get to the Berrystead.

Andrew Spurrell

11

David Gray, Florence Gray's father, with David Buckerfield by the garden gate at Brakehill Farm.

How Edgar Edis Got His Name

I was born in Titchmarsh in 1920 in the house I still live in. It used to have a thatched roof. My father became the tenant here in 1906. He went into the 1914-1918 war and when he came back he felt he would like a piece of extra land to have his hens and pigs on. He got the land with the agreement that a cart way should be between the garden and the extra piece so that there would be access to the field. This cottage belonged to the Lilford estate. When Lord Lilford died at the end of the Second World War, the estate was bought by the Bristol Merchant Venturers.

I had a brother, Edgar, who was born in 1906. He went to Laxton School for two or three years and he then went to work as a motor mechanic at Heighton's Garage in Elton. He used to cycle to Elton and he lodged there for the week and cycled back to Titchmarsh on a Friday night. He lodged with the manager of the garage at the time, a Mr Edis, and his wife was pregnant. When she had a baby boy they named him Edgar after my brother.

Raymond Gray

Tin Lizzy

My maiden name was Phyllis Essam and I was born in Islip. We lived at Hill Cottage and it was next door to Doctor Lascelles who was there for years and years. I had one brother, Bertram. My father, Charles Essam, had a hardware business. My mother was Susan Elizabeth Tooley before she married.

In those days everything was taken around in a horse and dray. Then the Tin Lizzy Ford came along. He ran the business from the cottage. We had three quarters of an acre of

A very young Andrew Spurrell with his older sister, Judith, c. 1940.

land and some outbuildings which were used as storage for things like paraffin.

Phyllis Whittaker

A Bit of Scrumping

When we were little, I was rather a nice looking child and my brother was a real boy. He had a friend about the same age and they used to say, come on, we're going scrumping. They gave me a penny to go into Mrs Boulter's shop at the end of Halford Street. This was a general store and I was instructed to ask for a ha'porth of aniseed balls and a ha'porth of floral gums. That was because one was at one top end of the sweet shelf and the other was at the other top end and Mrs Boulter had to get her steps to reach them. It meant she was a long time serving me (but she still gave me a sugar mouse) and my brother and his friend collected some apples and pears from her garden.

We would put on our roller skates and wait for a car or even a lorry to come along Huntingdon Road or the High Street. They would only be going at fifteen or twenty miles and hour so you grabbed hold of the back and be pulled along.

We used to put night lines out. You put a stake out of sight in the river bank and attached to it was a line. There were two or three strong hooks baited with large worms dug from the garden and a weight on the end. We threw it out in the river and early in the morning – sometimes it was very early and we used to climb out of the bedroom window and down the drainpipe to get to the river by five o'clock. We used to haul the line in and have two or three eels and then sell them to the landlord of one of the pubs.

We used to poach rabbits in the fields round the back of Market Road that were owned by old Mr Bletsoe and also down in

Annie Gray (centre), Raymond Gray's mother taking tea in the back garden at Titchmarsh. The boy standing is William Edgar Gray who tragically drowned in the river at Elton in 1924.

Philip Loaring, aged five.

the meadows. We used to bring them home and my mother used to skin and cook them.

Philip Loaring

Born at the Top End

I was born at the top end of the village in No. 31 Barnwell. My granddad, George Marriott was born in Barnwell and so was my father, Percy. There was Trevor and me and we have an elder sister, Mary. My mother was called Violet.

Norah Blunt

Nursing Money

I remember going round with my mother and collecting the nursing money. I think it was a penny a week and people collected in dif-ferent streets. The money would pay for the District Nurse in the town.

Joyce Bird

A Wash House in the Garden

My mother was born in Duck Street in Elton. There were three cottages in a row and she was born in the middle one. Her name was Pridmore and my father's was Burgess. There is a white house just this side of the chapel and there used to be three cottages and my mother and father lived in the first one. It's a farmhouse now. There was just a sitting room and a little kitchen and quite a big garden. There was one bed-room and there was a big square landing and we used that as a bedroom. There was a wash house in the garden and a little yard. The privy was right at the top of the gar-den. People who lived in the row of cottages used to get together and dig a pit in the garden and get rid of everything. I had a brother and two sisters.

My dad used to drive threshing engines. He worked for Jack Sanders who had the farm opposite the post office.

Our mother used to make our clothes. We wore liberty bodices and garters to keep our socks up.

Dorothy Osborne

Extravagance

Our shop was next door to Goss's and Pru and I were friends. If we wanted to talk to each other, we would knock on the wall. I remember spending half a crown on buying a book from Pru's shop. It was *Little Grey*

Daniel Burgess, Dorothy Osborne's father, with one of the massive farm tractors, c. 1920.

Rabbit and when I got home my mother said I had been very extravagant and I didn't have any pocket money for two weeks!

Joyce Bird

A Large Family

We lived in a house that was at the back of the new Co-op Extra car park. There were three houses with wrought iron railings and a passage down the side and we lived at the back. There were fifteen of us in our family. My mother's maiden name was Craythorne. There were nine girls and dad was very strict with us. Dad was a bookmaker's clerk where Owen and Hartley is now. Everybody loved him but he did like the drink so my mother brought us up. When the war came, he had to go and do a job he didn't like which was driving a lorry. My mother used to work hard and always seemed to be doing the washing in the outhouse. Our toilet was right up at the back of the garden. I have never eaten runner beans since because dad used to grow them up the wire which was hung against the toilet. Every Saturday we used to help clean the house.

Audrey Knight

No Library Books

As children we were not allowed to have library books from either Wellingborough or Kettering, both of which were seven miles away. It was believed in those days that you could pick up germs from library books.

Mary Thomson

Josiah Hilliard, Wilfred Osborne's grandfather, who was a coachman for the Probys at Elton Hall.

Born in Islip

I was born in the first house in West Yard, Islip opposite the Rose and Crown. It has been knocked down and made into stables for Wadenhoe Mill. I left Islip when I was twelve after losing my mother and I went to Lowick where I stayed until I was twenty-seven.

John Jeffs

Hups and Downs

When I was quite young I was walking around the village one morning. Anyone I met I more or less knew. I said politely to one person; 'Good morning, how are you?' thinking I was so grown up to say 'how are you?'. She replied; 'Well, me dear, I have me hups and downs, y'know.' I didn't know what she meant by 'hups' so I had to ask my mother!

Phyllis Whittaker

A Crafty Smoke

At the bottom of Ship Lane there are some fields that now belong to Oundle School but used to belong to Mr Rowell who had the dairy. We were allowed to go in there and play down by the backwater. Some of my friends used to go and have a crafty smoke!

Ann Cheney

Catching Tiddlers

We used to go down to the Jubilee bridges. You go down Riverside Close and if you go as though you are going across the fields you see two bridges. They were little wooden bridges. We used to take a jam jar and a bit of string to catch tiddlers.

Jill Fletcher

The Roaring Wash

We played all sorts of games when we were children – whip and top, hop scotch – and we used to play in the middle of the road because there was so little traffic. I played with Muriel Lovett who was my special friend. We used to play in the river, where the eel traps are now. We called it The Scolopit and we used to have diving boards. There was an overflow that used to run into a dyke on the edge of a field near the mill. We called it the Roaring Wash.

Dorothy Osborne

Dorothy Burgess, now Osborne, in Elton, c. 1925.

Early Decisions

Lower Farm was a dairy farm but we had sheep and pigs. I decided at a very early age that I was not going to learn to milk a cow. They had to be milked twice a day come whatever. I also decided I was not going to learn to drive a car while I was at home. The one that drove the car was the one who had to go at a moments notice to fetch something for the tractor when it broke down, or run here or there and get something or do something. It interrupted one's social life, I decided. My sister Mary was always aggravated because she had learned to drive.

Norah Blunt

Uneven Slabs

We lived in a farmhouse and I had to do all sorts of things when I was a girl. I had to wash the kitchen floor for a start and that wasn't easy because there were great, uneven slabs.

I had a bucket of water, a scrubbing brush and soap. The soap used to be bought and then put in the cupboard to dry out so it was really hard. It was hard, yellow soap.

Norah Blunt

Earning a Badge

Brownies were held at The British School along West Street. Miss Bolt, who was the matron at one of the schools, was the Brown Owl and her assistant was Mrs Cauldwell whose husband was a housemaster at the school. I can't remember much about it except I had to go to somebody's house in Milton road to lay the table so I could earn one of the badges.

Ann Cheney

Summer 1944 at Lower Farm, Barnwell with Fred Lewis (top) and Mary Brow, Percy Marriott and Mary Marriott (centre), Norah Marriott (front) and unknown girl 'staying next door'.

CHAPTER 2

House and Home

Barnwell church with the girls' school still in the churchyard. This was taken down and erected later beside the Manor and was known as Bigley's Bungalow.

Making a Feather Bed

We had feather beds on top of hard mattresses and my mother used to make them herself. They were made from a long piece of material, ticking, filled with feathers. As you killed the birds – usually chickens but we did have geese and ducks – the feathers were put in a newspaper and rolled into a bundle and tied at the ends and then put on a rack above the fireplace. They stayed there until they dried out and then were taken upstairs and kept in a dark room. When my mother wanted to make a new pillow or bed she would strip the feathers from the spines. She needed at least a year's supply. Below our kitchen at the back there was a dairy that we didn't use and my mother would go by herself with the feathers and the material because she could be quiet in there.

Florence Gray

Filling the Water Tank

In Barnwell there were, and still are, a lot of wells but they've been blocked up. When there was a water shortage up the farm, we used to go down with a horse and cart with a big tank on the back. Opposite where you used to live at No. 8 Barnwell, there was a pump by the side of the bridge, and we would fill up with water from that pump, putting it into buckets and then into the tank, and taking it back to Lower Farm for the cattle. Nearly everybody had their own well when I was young.

Norah Blunt

Helping in the House

I left school when I was fifteen and stayed at home for the next four years. I helped with the dairy work twice a day, cleaning the dairy. It was very early. A man used to come with a pony and cart to take the milk away and he was always at the farm by about seven thirty in the morning. By nine o'clock there were all the buckets, the cooler and the strainer to clean and sterilise. We had to do the same thing in the evening. The milking was finished by half past four to five.

We had a very large house and no help. There were six bedrooms and two attic rooms. There was no electricity and we used oil lamps. We cleaned windows with water and crumpled-up newspapers.

We would do the washing on Mondays. There were no washing machines and we used a copper that stood in the corner of the wash house and we would soak things before we washed them. The soap came in big slabs and you bought it from the grocer. You had a wire with a little handle each side and you cut it into squares. We had a big, black 'Kitchener' and either side there were little cupboards and there you put your soap to dry. If things were really dirty you boiled them in the copper and they came out clean. Everything was either

Sisters Mary (now Thomson) and Jean (now Yarnold) Howard at Great Addington in 1938.

linen or cotton or wool. There were no synthetic things.

There was a big stone sink that had to be scrubbed clean when we had used it and a galvanised tub with two handles. We didn't have any sinks in the kitchen. There was the kitchen stove and a big table. There was a row of bells, seven or eight, which were connected to the rooms in the house. There were also hooks for hanging up the hams.

Mary Thomson

Seventy-three Years in Cotterstock

I was thirteen when we moved to Cotterstock from Apethorpe. I didn't go to school after that. I have lived in the village for longer than anyone else – for seventy-three years. Gladys is next as she has lived here for fifty-four years.

Harold Ashby

Always the 'Blue Bag'

Wash day was always Monday and we always had cold dinner with vegetables fried up from Sunday. To do the washing, you'd take the water from the pump in a bucket and carry it to the wash house and fill the copper. The copper had a fire underneath to heat it and you used to save old cardboard boxes to burn. My mum used to use that yellow soap and soda and there was always the 'blue-bag' to keep things white. When things had to be starched you had to mix up the powder with boiling water.

We had a cooking range, one with a fire in the middle with a boiler one side and oven the other. We had lots of suet puddings, roly-poly puddings and things like that. We didn't get electricity in Chapel Lane until after the war.

In those days the floor was made up of bricks and we had pegged rugs.

Kept Warm by the Fire

The high spot of my week, I remember, was when I came home on a Tuesday and my mother had always kept some of the mince and the potatoes and the peas. It was always potatoes and peas with the mince and it was put in a basin by the fire. We had a wonderfully cool pantry.

Pru Goss

A Job for Everyone

My dad, William Norwood, was the blacksmith at No. 42 Barnwell. I was born at Thurning because he worked with his father at Thurning and then when Barnwell became vacant in 1910 they moved from

Number 8 Barnwell, the old estate yard house, where the carpenter, Mr Maddison lived. The thatched cottage in the front was always known in the village as Mrs Best's house. The tree in the centre has long since disappeared.

Thurning to Barnwell. My name was Norwood then. Reg Norwood who had the taxi service in Oundle was my cousin. I think Carl Norwood is the only Norwood left now.

There were five of us and we were a happy family. We all had our jobs to do in the house, helping with the washing up and cleaning the cutlery and the brass on a Saturday. Often mother put the knives in a knife machine and turned the handle and that would clean them. They were steel knives in those days. Mother's name was Florence Lofts before she married my father and she came from Little Downham in Cambridgeshire. I think she used to work at Thurning rectory as a lady's maid.

We used to have two cows and mother used to make butter. She sold it to a grocer who came from Thrapston. My father had a little field right down Polebrook road and he used to have to lay that for hay. They used to have a cowkeeper and he used to mind the cows on the roadside every day in the summertime. His name was William Ogilvy and his brother had a shop next to the Chancel. There used to be two cottages there but Mr Kisby turned it into one. I remember mum going up there and buying stockings. I think they sold drapery and all sorts of things but it was closed when I was quite young.

Eileen Woolman

No Garden

We lived above the shop in New Street and we didn't have a garden, we had what we called two yards. There was the big yard which belonged to us but which the post office, and the premises next door, which I remember were jewellers, had a right of way over, and there was a smaller yard.

Ann Cheney

Lucy Burgess, nee Pridmore, of Elton.

Once a Rubbish Dump

Harold and I were engaged in 1945, we married in 1946, we moved in here in 1947 and Joyce was born in 1948. At first we just had half the land we have now and then we bought another field. Altogether we have about four and a half acres, perhaps a little more. Harold bought the first bit, which was about two acres, for £50 and three years after I bought the field for £200. It sounds cheap now but it was a lot of money in those days. Harold had bought this field and it was a rubbish dump. He borrowed a horse and a plough and cleaned it all. He sowed it with potatoes to clean the land – they were no good at all – but he cleaned the land before we built the house. After that, he made the plans, in triplicate.

Gladys Ashby

21

Sally the monkey.

Bags of Potatoes

I had the land in Cotterstock for about five years before we were married. After I'd cleared the land and grown potatoes, we couldn't sell them because, grown on grassland or rubbish land, they were full of wireworm. I took them down to Mr Rowell's, who had the dairy farm at Oundle. He had pigs and I took him the potatoes, three or four bags at a time.

Harold Ashby

Penny a Peep!

My brother brought a monkey called Sally back in a case and when he opened it the monkey jumped out, got onto the table where there were some apples, grabbed one in each hand and bit them and then ran off. My mother was horrified! This was during the war and I used to charge people a penny to come and look at the monkey. When I'd collected five pounds I sent it to Mrs Churchill for the Russians.

Anne Beesley

Annoying the Cat

Percy Brookfield was a merchant navy man and he brought home a monkey. This monkey used to sit on the boiler and his prime object was to annoy the cat! The Brookfields had a beautiful, big, black and white cat and when it had almost disappeared into the living room, the monkey used to jump off the boiler, grab hold of the cat's tail, tweak it and jump back on the boiler again. This used to annoy the cat and one day the cat walked very sedately by and then into the living room and as usual the monkey jumped down ready to tweak its tail. But the cat was ready! It scratched all across the monkey's face making it squeal and cry like a baby. The monkey didn't try and tweak the tail again after that!

Philip Loaring

Making Toilet Paper

One of our afternoon jobs was to cut newspaper into squares to use as toilet paper. We'd make a hole at the corner and threading several pieces on a piece of string. In those days there was horrible Bronco toilet paper, too.

Joyce Bird

Shut Doors and Windows

I came to Thrapston in 1957 and my wife Jean and I came to live in this house in

Cottages in Oundle Road, Thrapston, that were demolished around 1926.

Oundle Road which belonged to her parents. Jean's parents were Florence and Reg Brinsley. Florence was a local but Reg came from Oundle.

Before the bypass, if you lived on the Oundle road in Thrapston, you couldn't leave your windows or doors open on a warm day because there was so much traffic. There were no traffic lights and so it was everybody for themselves at the junction. It was the same over the bridge but in the narrow part where the fire station is now they did put in lights.

Eddie Rowe

Suffolk Cooks are the Best

My mother was a very good cook. She came from Suffolk and always said that the best cooks came from Suffolk! She cooked all the things that nowadays are considered bad for you! She made steak and kidney puddings and pies, plenty of good pastry, rabbit pies and chicken pies and of course, all fruit pies. My father, as well as having an allotment, had an enormous garden at the back of the shop. We had blackcurrant bushes, gooseberry bushes, strawberries and raspberries.

Philip Loaring

A Drudgery

We were two miles from the butcher and would buy our meat on Saturdays. We were two miles from Sudborough and two miles from Brigstock. I stayed at the farm and I did the housework. My eldest sister, from the age of twelve, milked four cows every day. Housework in those days was a drudgery. I had to make the beds of my sisters and myself. You had to shake the feathers and spread the feathers out flat. We also had a long bolster that went across the top of the bed and you would put your pillows on top of that.

Florence Gray

Building the House

When I had drawn the plans for our house in Cotterstock I took them to the planners. They weren't keen on some things. They altered the angle of the roof and I didn't agree with that but I had to do it. I dug the foundations out by hand and to build I used to fetch Joe Edwards, a bricklayer from Titchmarsh, every morning. It was for four mornings a week. Harry Foster, who was a haulage contractor, brought me loads of concrete off Polebrook aerodrome. Harry lived up Benefield Road in Oundle. Joe did the outside brickwork and I did inside. We got as far as the roof and then Joe wouldn't risk scrambling about up there (he was elderly) so I put the roof on by myself, but Gladys carried the tiles up for me.
It took us about two years by the time I'd finished.

Harold Ashby

Yorkshire Round the Joint

When I was a child we took the Sunday lunch to the bakehouse to be cooked. We would take it when we went to church and collect it when we came out. Father used to take a big tin with a joint of roast beef and the Yorkshire pudding put round it.

Eileen Woolman

No Work on Sundays

There was a brickyard up Thurning road and there used to be a lime kiln on the Armston road and a gravel pit up Toot Hill at the top end of the village. Down by the Manor there was Empty Spinney and there is one further down on the Polebrook corner called the Sweatly Spinney. There used to be a bridge there over the brook and you could walk up over another black bridge and out on to the Oundle Road. We often used to go there on a Sunday afternoon walk. Dad used to meet us after Sunday school and take us for a walk.

We used to go to Sunday School at ten o'clock then to church at eleven. We went back to Sunday school at two o'clock and mum and dad would meet us out at three o'clock. We were not allowed to do anything on a Sunday. We could read but we were not allowed to knit.

Saturday night used to be bath night and dad used to put our hair all in rags to make ringlets on Sunday. The bath was a big hip bath in front of the fire. There were three of us and we all had long hair. On Sunday it was in ringlets but on other days it was plaited at the back.

Eileen Woolman

Keeping a Pig

We kept our own pig and we used to take it to be butchered. There were two butchers in the village then. Years ago, it was Mr Knight who was up the hill on the right. There was also a Mr Chamberlain who was a butcher. When the pig was butchered we would hang up the hams. They would be salted, rubbed all over with salt.

Raymond Gray

No Water, No Electricity

I met my husband at a dance at the Victoria Hall. I was nineteen and I liked him because he was very smart. He wasn't pushy at all and I liked that. I was wearing a short beige dress with chocolate coloured trimming. I was twenty-one when I married him. He worked as a charge-hand at Perkins which was a good job. We lived with Gordon's sister in Peterborough for a while and then we were at Ashton having a drink and someone told us about this house and we have been here all the time. When we saw it there was no water and no electricity. That was in the early 1950s. It cost us £850. The house was a tip but Gordon was so clever and so calm that everything I asked him to do, he could. I said to him one day that I'd love to leave the office and have a little shop of my own. He said he thought he could apply for permission to change the front into a shop and he did. We sold everything. We had it for over twenty years.

Audrey Knight

Taking home the Sunday dinner from the bakehouse in Barnwell.

25

Numbers 29-32 Barnwell. According to Norah Blunt (nee Marriott) who was born at No. 31, the four cottages were once all one farmhouse.

A Tradition

It was a tradition to go and collect watercress from Barnwell brook. I would go with my father, Walter Woolman, on a Sunday afternoon. We also used to go and shoot pigeons and duck and we still have the decoys we used. Each house had its own well or access to a well so there were rights of way around the back. There was once a tremendous fire at the top end of the village and that was one of the reasons why my father would not seal our well up. He said that if there was a thatch fire near here then there would always be access to water. When it was very hot and before we had a fridge, we used the well to keep the meat cool. We put it in a basket on a rope.

Most of the wells were about a long handle depth. You had a hook on the end and hooked your bucket on and dropped it down and fetched the water up. The wells were in a line on each side of the road because the rock comes right down. The water was really quite pure because it was in the limestone. Barnwell brook used to be almost the width of the two roads, and just opposite my mother's house are stepping stones. When they put the gas in the village they wondered what they had hit. They thought it was rock. The septic tanks used to empty into the brook. I think it was on main drainage in 1972.

The stepping stones were replaced by two tree trunks with planks nailed on them. There were no street lights so at night we used to find the end of the bridge by walking towards the lime tree and then you used your foot to ascertain exactly where the pegs were in the ground that held the planks in. Then you shot across in a straight line. We never fell in although people used to say that you were never real members of the community until you had fallen in!

Susan Pearson

Still in Use

I put the stove in – it's an Ideal Cookanheat no. 35 – and we still use it. I used to send to the firm for spare parts and the last time I heard the firm had closed down so there were no more spares. Now we have to rely on local firms and I make the firebricks. Anything that goes wrong I have to make it.

Harold Ashby

Dusting the Bannisters

My first job as a very small child was to dust the banisters every Saturday morning. There were thirteen or fourteen going up the stairs and about the same number going along the landing. I rather liked doing it.

Mary Thomson

Everybody Helped

During the war we had a pig co-operative and we applied for a pig slaughter licence. When the pigs were slaughtered, everybody – and I mean *everybody* – was out there salting down the bacon and making sausages. One of my jobs was to clean the small intestines with the back of a knife and get all the gunge out until they were a long, continuous skin. You would thread it on to a nozzle on the mincing machine, tie a knot in the end and turn the handle and feed the meat through, every

now and then giving a twist. And weren't they lovely sausages!

Philip Loaring

Home Cooking

My mother often made big jam tarts, ones that covered a plate. We used to eat rabbit and on some occasions we would have a pigeon pie. We had different ways of cooking a rabbit. If you were roasting it you would take off the head before to make the gravy and the rest of it would go in the oven. There would be two joints from the back legs, three from the back and two shoulders. Then we had rabbit stew. Sometimes we had lamb but my father was very soft hearted and didn't like killing them. We also ate chicken and duck.

We grew beans and lines and lines of peas that we set every fortnight so they would last us. We grew cabbages and swedes.

My grandfather was David Gray, the same name as my father. He was a shepherd on Lord Barnard's estate at Sudborough and he was born in 1820. My father took over the farm around 1890.

Florence Gray

The Fire

There was an electrical fault and we had a terrible fire. That was sometime in the 1970s. I had gone to stay with Dorothy Brudenell and we had a phone call at eleven at night to say the house was on fire. When I got there you could see the water coming down New Road and there were crowds of people.

Audrey Knight

Nurse Carry Bream was the district nurse for Nassington and Yarwell during the 1920s.

First Home

We had a shop in Yarwell. I ran the post office and shop in the centre of the village for eighteen years when we were first married. That was our first home. It was just a post office to start with and then we started selling birthday cards and Christmas cards. There was one other shop.

We had that, the mill herd, the mill farm and the mill. At that time the village had two pubs, The Angel and The Fox and there were a lot of thatched cottages.

Grace Starsmore

A Useful Screen

We had the first colour television! It was a screen that you put in front of the television and at the top it was blue, then green and then brown at the bottom!

Anne Beesley

A Bath in Front of the Range

The cottage had four bedrooms, a dining room, drawing room, breakfast room and a large pantry. There was a lean-to greenhouse through to the kitchen. There wasn't a bathroom although we had one put in, in 1944. We had a galvanised bath, full length, that was hung up in one of the outbuildings. It was brought into the house on bath night. In the kitchen, which was quite big, there was a copper and underneath what they called a copper hole where you put the fuel. There was a tap (and believe it or not, a little drain) and that had soft water and so you filled the copper from that. The bath was put in front of the range in the kitchen and when you had finished with it, you emptied it into the drain.

My mother had help in the house. Violet Bigley lived in and she came from Pilton. She had a deformed shoulder blade.

Phyllis Whittaker

Six Cottages

Our farm in Great Addington had six cottages that went with it. Two were down towards the meadows and there were four opposite the house.

Mary Thomson

Home Farm at Great Addington, taken from the south in the 1920s.

The Dark Room

Our farmhouse was thatched and there was a dark room which had a window looking into the next room and you could see out of that room's window but nobody could see you. On a clear day you could see straight through to Desborough which was five miles away.

In the parlour there was a carpet and we cleaned that once a week with a stiff brush and went over it again with a soft brush. I liked polishing the furniture and we used a furniture cream. It hasn't changed very much in the last years. If you polished it properly after you had put the cream on then there would be no polish left.

Florence Gray

Good to Eat

I think hock 'n' dough is a traditional local dish. They call the football team at Wellingborough The Dough Boys. The dough is the pastry that you put in the bottom of the tin and the hock is the pork.

The way my mother used to make it – which is the way I have continued to make it – is by first making a suet crust pastry. In those days you had to grate the suet yourself, there was no ready-made packets. You had a big roasting tin that you lined completely with the pastry and let it overlap the sides. Then you would put in the pork, which could be chops or pork cuttings or a hock. Over the meat you spread onions. My mother didn't chop them finely but cut them roughly. She did the same with potatoes and put them on top of the onions, seasoning well with pepper. Then you make up a Bisto gravy – it has to be Bisto! – and pour it around and then put the whole thing in a very, very hot oven to bring it to the boil. Turn it down very low and leave it in for four or five hours. The people who worked in the factories would put it in the oven in the morning before they went to work and then when they came home midday it was ready to eat. You had to be careful to leave enough liquid in because it could become dry.

My friend Daphne Bilson makes it a different way. She makes shortcrust pastry and she browns her meat, puts the onions in raw, and parboils the potatoes which she then sprinkles with flour.

Jean Woodward

Practice Made Perfect

I played the piano for six hours every day when I was doing my LRAM. I also played the violin and the 'cello. I went on to teach in several schools around the country when I left home.

Florence Gray

Looking Over the Station

My daughter used the railway every day to go to school in Wellingborough. It was the only way to get there. From my house in Glapthorn Road I could sit in the garden and see the railway station and watch the train come in. There wasn't one house between our garden and the railway station. And when we saw the train in the afternoon, we knew that my daughter would be here in ten minutes time.

Reg Sutton

Between Two Companies

We hadn't electricity in the early days because we were between the two companies – the East Midlands Electricity and Eastern Electricity – and neither company wanted to bring the electricity quite a distance – from Tansor to Elmington or Oundle to Elmington – just for half a dozen properties.

John Preston

Lack of Housing

When I was on the council in the 1960s, there was a complete lack of houses for people. In Inkerman Yard, there were twenty-four families living there. They had no back doors and only a big, communal toilet. There was no electric light or gas inside the house and no running water.

Reg Sutton

A Good Polishing

Once a year we would wash the furniture with vinegar and water and then polish it well. That polishing would last a year. As a child, I remember the carpets, which were square and went on to the floor so that there was the varnished wood floorboards around the outside. Even in the attic bedrooms, in the spring or early summer, every carpet was taken up, taken down onto the lawn and beaten. They were put flat on the lawn and beaten. The centres of the floors, which were unvarnished because they were covered by the carpets, were then scrubbed. The curtains were also taken down and washed.

Mary Thomson

Not Just Beer for Sale

My grandfather lived at The Black Horse in Tansor. That was the family home. There were several generations of Prestons living there. It was a unique situation where they sold milk, butter, eggs and beer from the same counter.

John Preston

Cleaning Out the Ashes

When I left school I would get up and light the fires. The big old 'Kitchener' in the kitchen had to have the ashes cleaned out every morning. I had to get up before six, get the fire going and have a cup of tea

Philip and Mary Preston.

Glapthorn Road, Oundle.

waiting for my father when he come down. He would then go out and set the men to work and come back for breakfast about eight o'clock.

We would have porridge for breakfast, followed by bacon or most probably home-cured ham and there would be honey because my father kept bees. We had bread but not toast.

I cooked for all the family, too. On Sundays we always had a joint – lamb, or beef or pork. The butcher used to call once a week because he came from Woodford. His name was Thomas Ward. He was a neat man with a neat moustache and was rather military-looking. There was a baker in Great Addington, Mr Wright. His wife kept the post office. All the people living in the village were either farm workers or boot and shoe workers, and did not have a lot of money. I remember they used to have 27s 6d a week wages if they worked on the farms. However on Sundays most people would have a small joint. They used to put the batter pudding and the joint and the potatoes around it in a baking tin and take it to the bakehouse about ten o'clock and they would go and collect it about one o'clock.

An aerial view of Great Addington showing Home Farm, where the Howard family lived, in the foreground. The Ringstead road leads off to the right, and at the top of the picture, the road forks near the church towards Kettering and Woodford.

A Robin for Princess Alice

Mary Thomson

Every Christmas I have embroidered Princess Alice a Christmas card with a robin on it. One Christmas I thought I wouldn't bother but she said to me how she looked forward to getting my little robin each year so I thought I had better carry on!

Norah Blunt

Caring for Over Fifty Years

Oundle and District Care Committee was started in 1949 and Tom Cunnington was the chairman. They used to provide milk to poor people, many who had TB. We have always raised money by having a Spring Fair and a Christmas Appeal. We changed from giving milk to providing Christmas parcels to mostly single, old age pensioners who had little or no income. They were made up of sugar and tea and biscuits and all the things you get at Christmas time.

Over the years we have built up a lot of loan equipment for people to borrow free of charge. Now we have fifteen wheelchairs in Oundle and all sorts of other medical equipment.

Reg Sutton

CHAPTER 3
Schooldays

A class at Elton school taken in the schoolyard, c. 1926. Dorothy Burgess is on the left in the front row and her future husband, Wilfred Osborne, is in the top row on the right.

Singing Hymns

I went first to Miss Webb's school, St Christopher's School in Oundle, until I was eight. Miss Connie Webb ran the school. It was near where Ashton Estate is now. You go past the council houses, there are one or two new houses and then there is a turning. You go up there and there is a big house. My sister, my brother and my son all went to Miss Webb's. When we were young we used to cut across the fields to get to school. Opposite the Co-op car park there was an opening and we would cut through there. There were some fields that belonged to Button Horn and he had ponies. We would go through

Campbell House School at Higham Ferrars, which was owned by Miss Payne in the 1920s. From left to right, back row: Joan Adams, Nora ?, -?-, -?-, Margaret Beeby. Centre: -?-, Barbara Russell, Peggy Howard. Front row: -?-, Hilda Hawkes.

there and into Miss Webb's field.

Miss Webb always looked the same to me, even when my son Stephen went to school. She had very dark hair with a centre parting and curled into 'earphones' each side of her head. I suppose she was about five foot four or five and she was thin. Her father, I believe, was the station master at Oundle at one time. We did reading, writing and arithmetic. We had to learn our tables and learn our spellings. I can remember standing round the piano in the mornings and singing hymns.

Ann Cheney

A Dame School

We had governesses until I was twelve and then I went to school in Heigham Ferrars

until I was fifteen. It was a dame school called Campbell House. It was run by a lady who had once had a school in Switzerland, at Neuchatel, I think, and she was absolutely crippled with rheumatism which is why she came back to England. It was on the south side of the square and in a tall, three-story house. She took girls – and boys until they were about six – but there was no sixth form so the girls at that stage went elsewhere, either to Bedford High School or a place at Felixstowe.

Mary Thomson

Laxton and Oundle

I was at Laxton School and when I was there the master in charge was Sidney Leech and the headmaster of Oundle School at that time was known as 'Bud' Fisher. His son is the ornithologist, James Fisher. When I was there Laxton was only partially integrated into Oundle School. If you had your School Certificate and you were sitting your Higher, then you would take lessons with Oundle School pupils. Laxton boys were taught by Oundle School staff.

Philip Brudenell

Standards

I was born in a house called The Poplars in Oundle Road, Thrapston and we lived there until 1939. I went to school in Huntingdon Road and then on to Kettering High School. At Huntingdon Road school the head teacher was Mr Williams and he was very strict. He was a smallish man and Welsh. When the evacuees arrived in 1941, they didn't have our standards of discipline and

he used to get very cross and they were always having the cane.

Anne Beesley

Better Prospects

I came to teach at Oundle School in 1949. They offered me a bigger salary, more chance of promotion and the amenities were better. The only reason I was appointed was because of my wartime experiences as an interrogator in MI5. Immediately after the war I made all sorts of applications to different schools and I told them what I had done in the war. Some of the schools were frightened but Graham Stainforth who was the headmaster of Oundle School, came from a military family and understood what I had done during the war. So I joined the school as a Spanish master.

In those days they were all rugby players

The Poplars in 1938.

Nassington School, probably taken in 1928. Jack Starsmore is fourth from the left in the back row standing next to Jerry Hollowell. Jack Mould is seated on the floor on the right.

and all cricket players. Quite early on the headmaster was trying to improve the teaching of English in the school and because I had come from a grammar school he asked me if the boys at Oundle were as good at English as those at the grammar school. I said the grammar school boys were better! So he put me in charge of the school magazine.

I spent four years as a house tutor to 'Tub' Shaw in Sydney House.

Alec Payne

Changing Trains

When I was a boy I first went to Nassington School and then to Laxton in Oundle. We lived at Willowbrook Farm and I went to Laxton School by train. I took the train from Nassington to Wansford and changed to the Northampton line which went on to Oundle.

Jack Starsmore

Not Her Favourite Lesson

Our headmaster, Sammy Reynolds, was very jingoistic and he ran the school, Wollaston Primary on military lines. He was a very, very strict disciplinarian. I started in the infants' school at three years old. I remember Miss Summerlin was one teacher. I hated needlework. We had to do samples. If you were very good you made garments but I was never any good and I only ever did run and fell seams – and I had to unpick most of those! Mavis Austin was a friend of mine and her father was a gardener at Wollaston Hall which even then

Wellingborough High School performs a pageant on the theme 'Women through the Ages' in 1951. Jean Pearson (now Woodward) took the role of Queen Elizabeth.

was Scott Bader. We used to play in the Spinney where we used to get wild plums. Mavis's father used to grow wonderful tomatoes and lots of vegetables. They had a canning machine and while everybody else used to bottle fruit, they used to can it!

Jean Woodward

By Train and Bicycle

I went to Elton C of E school. There was Sarah and Mary Brawn and Miss Lloyd who used to teach the infants. Sarah Brawn was the head teacher. Miss Lloyd used to live in Thrapston and she used to come to Elton by train every day and cycle up to school from the station. When she went home she would leave her cycle at the station. The first station master I can remember at Elton was Mr Brooks. Then there was Mr Knibbs.

Dorothy Osborne

Writing Practice

There were about twenty or thirty in a class at Wollaston. We each had a desk and they were in rows. We had pens we had to dip into inkwells and we used to do writing practice. There were big charts on the walls with capitals and lower case and we copied them into exercise books.

I went to the High School at Wellingborough. Everybody who passed went there and we had girls from Polebrook and Oundle and Thrapston.

Jean Woodward

Two Teachers, One Room

I went to school in Grafton Underwood. There were never more than thirty-six children and there were two teachers in one big room. The headmistress, who was called Mrs Linnell, took children from the age of about eight. She was not very tall and she was plump.

We always started the day with prayers and the first lesson was scripture and what we had to do was sent from the diocese in Peterborough. Once a year they would come round and examine us.

At midday we would sit on a long form in front of the fire and eat our sandwiches. Sometimes my mother would make a little pudding for us. We had our main meal when we got home. It was left over from the one o'clock dinner the men had and mother would put our meal aside and heat it up for us later. We usually got home between half past three and quarter to four. Sometimes we would have toad in the hole which was slices of meat put in a batter pudding.

Florence Gray

Ink in Stone Bottles

When I was at school we learned history and geography. We had desks with an inkwell and the ink came in big stone bottles. We always went home for lunch.

Pru Goss

Music Makers

Sanderson was very fond of music and as a result the school choir used to sing the Bach B minor Mass and about every four years they performed it in Peterborough Cathedral. Because he was so well known, he was able to persuade eminent artists to come and sing the solo roles almost free of charge.

We also had a 'non-choir' made up of boys who were not good singers. They used to

make an enormous, electrifying sound.

Alec Payne

Beacon Readers

I went to school at Miss Hill's in Thrapston. It was at No. 119 Huntingdon Road and there were only nine of us there and we were there from aged four to aged eight. There were two Miss Hills, but one used to do the housework. Old Mrs Hill, the mother, lived in the main part of the house and we used a little room at the back. We had a chalk board to write on and we learnt such things as when Empire Day was – which was 24 May. We always dressed up on that day. I remember reading from a Beacon Reader about Old Lobb.

Joyce Bird

Helen (later Lenton) and Marjorie (later Spurrell) Cheney when they were at Townley House School in Oundle.

Andrew Spurrell (right) and his brother, Roworth.

Jumping the Seam

We had mental arithmetic and there was a rush carpet with a seam down the middle. You stood on one side and if you got the sum correct you were allowed to jump over the seam to the other. If you got the next one right you jumped back.

Joyce Bird

Pulling Faces

When we were punished we had to stand on the seat. This meant you could see through the glass partition into the next classroom. If you were careful not to be caught by your teacher, you could make faces at children in the next room and get them into trouble!

Pru Goss

Patriotic Songs

We used to walk about three-quarters of a mile to the organist's home. Her name was Mrs Medcroft. She lived in Oundle Road and she taught us singing. We learnt patriotic songs like *The British Grenadiers*, *Men of Harlech* and *Hearts of Oak*. I think we went through a book of national songs. We had to go, even if it was pouring with rain.

Joyce Bird

Our Own School

During the war we had our own school just at the back of Queen Anne's. The teacher was Miss Oliver. Edwin Streather came to school there, so did Christopher and Barry Capron. There were about a dozen of us. Later, I went to the redcap school, St

Christopher's School, also known as Miss Webb's. All the Howard family went there, the Richardsons, the Singlehursts, the Lights, the Gents, John Allman and Peter Clarke were there. Some of the people I went to school with were not very bright – and still aren't! Some of them were very clever and should have gone on further.

Andrew Spurrell

Walking to School

I was at Tansor School during the war. I started there when I was five and Miss Kay was the headmistress. She was there from 1936 to 1952. She lived at No. 40, North Street in Oundle and she used to walk to the school in Tansor every day. She very kindly used to pick me up at Tansor Lodge Cottage and I would walk with her to school. At lunchtime I used to walk home by myself. It was about a mile.

I sat next to Geoffrey Richards and the Rootham family used to come to school too. Bill Rootham was the gardener at Tansor Manor. The Sumners also came. They lived in Elm House in the middle of the village. Charles Sumner was a coal merchant and he ran his business from Elton Station. Marjorie Sumner, his widow, moved to Warmington.

John Preston

Real Candles

At Christmas all the children had a party at school. There was always a big Christmas tree and it used to have real, lit candles on it. The head gardener from the Castle, Mr Mann, who was a crotchety old thing at times, used to have to stand there beside it with a little sponge at the end of a long cane and when the candles got low he used to put them out.

We used to have tea in the school and then we all had a present.

Norah Blunt

A Slight Informality

I had four years as a house tutor in Sydney House where the housemaster was 'Tub' Shaw. I had been brought up to call masters 'sir' and on the first Sunday I was in Oundle School I had to go and see him. I walked in past some walnut trees and there was a ladder with a boy at the bottom and a commotion at the top. I said to the boy: 'Can you direct me to Mr Shaw's study?' and he called out: 'Tub, you're wanted.' The master was up the tree getting walnuts. That informality was only in Sydney House. Everywhere else was very formal and the discipline was rigorous.

Alec Payne

Very Large Classes

When I came to Oundle, the educational system in this area was absolutely dire. If you had money and you could pay for it, you were all right. There was Laxton or Stamford School. When my daughter passed the 11 plus she had to travel to Wellingborough which was the nearest school. Three girls were able to pass the 11 plus and the rest had to go to the Secondary Modern School in West Street. There, they finished their education at fifteen and did no external examinations. If you wanted any further education you had to go to Corby Technical

Children and teachers at he British School in Oundle.

College or Peterborough.

When my daughter passed the 11 plus there were fifty-three children in her class. The desks were so tightly packed together, the teacher couldn't get through them so he got up on the top of the desks and walked around the sides of the classroom looking at the work. That was at Oundle Primary School on the corner of Drumming Well Lane and Milton Road.

My son passed his 11 plus two years later and there was only forty-eight in his class! In those days, not only did you have to pass the 11 plus, if you were a boy, you then had to pass the entrance examination to Laxton School. Laxton School was the only secondary, grammar school education you could get around here. If you passed their examination, then the county would pay the fees for you to go there.

Reg Sutton

Strict but Kind

I went to a preparatory school in Thrapston. It was owned by Mrs Medcraft and was on the Oundle Road. Mrs Medcraft was strict but kind and thoughtful. She was fairly tall. She played the organ and gave piano lessons. Father used to drive us to school in a Bullnose Morris Cowley. We sat at a table for our lessons.

When I was nine I went to the County High School at Wellingborough. I used to get up at half past six in the morning and mother used to cycle to the station with me. It was about a mile and I left my bicycle between the gravel pits entrance and the bridge. The train used to stop and take water near there. It travelled through from Peterborough to Northampton. The train left Thrapston at a quarter past seven and we got to Wellingborough just before eight o'clock. It was the best part of a mile to walk from the station to the school.

School dinners were some form of meat and two veg. There was suet pudding but it was more solid than the normal suet pudding. We also had a hot milk drink in the morning.

We wore navy gym tunics with white blouse and navy knickers. I had a pocket in my knicker leg. In that, I kept a little purse – which I've still got – and in that, the milk tickets. We bought the milk tickets on a Monday morning so we had them for the week.

Phyllis Whittaker

Being A Housemaster

When I was housemaster of Crosby House in the 1950s there were around forty-three boys. As a housemaster, you got up at half past seven and went to bed at eleven o'clock if you were lucky. If you were not teaching you were playing games – rugby or cricket.

All the teaching was done in the school – in the Cloisters, in the Science Block or in the 'Bungy' Palmer block for chemistry.

Originally, Crosby House was a bachelor house but I was married and we had two little girls so we had a 'Colt' cottage in the grounds. I used to go home at night and Miss Stevenson, the matron, looked after the House. She was very good; she was a dragon!

Speech Day was always in June. There was a boy called Jeremy Greenhalgh and his mother always had the best hat. It was voted the best hat by the staff and once I asked her how she managed it and she told me she took her husband and her boy to choose it!

After the speeches people would watch the cricket and go round the exhibitions. Every department put on an exhibition and the best one was always the science department under 'Bungy' Palmer.

Boys at Oundle School were only allowed to go into the town after two o'clock and never in school hours. Food was provided by the school tuck shop.

Alec Payne

Saving

At school we had to save 6d a week in National Savings. For that we got a stamp which we stuck on a card and when it reached £1 we had a certificate.

Anne Beesley

Oundle Primary School

I went to Oundle Primary School in Milton Road. I remember my teacher was Miss Streather. She was a lovely teacher. Then I went on to school in West Street. It was called Oundle County Modern School. Joyce Hardwick who was Joyce Gaunt was one of my friends and I used to go to school with her.

Audrey Knight

Catching Butterflies

We had to catch cabbage white butterflies when we were at school so that they wouldn't lay eggs and eat the cabbages.

Joyce Bird

Oundle Council School in West Street.

Changing for the Better

I realised that something had to be done about the education in Oundle. Because I hadn't any children going into the system, no-one could think I had a chip on my shoulder. I began to speak up at the parent-teacher meetings and I put up for the council to get my voice heard and got on. That was in 1958. By 1966 I became chairman of the council which gave me the opportunity to speak out on Oundle's behalf on various matters. I found out that the Urban District Council had little or no say about the provision of education. I called a public meeting to protest against the lack of education facilities in this area. It was packed. As a result we began to get moving and I was made the chairman of a delegation. The following year

there was a county council election and I realised that to do anything you had to be on the County Council. So there I was, completely independent and with no backing or funds, I put up as a candidate. My opponent was the Honourable George Brudenell from Deene but I was elected, much to the dismay of a lot of people. Once I was on the County Council, I got on the education committee and I was able to speak for the people of Oundle.

I had a big hand in getting a new school in the town. That happened in 1971 and we had to find a place to build it. It was planned that the site should be on the playing field the other side of The George, but Oundle School at that time needed more playing fields for educational purposes so that was ruled out. We searched around and came up with a plot on the outskirts of Herne Road and eventually we got twelve acres of land from Mr Ashby at Armston and Oundle Upper School opened. The official opening was by Prince William of Gloucester in 1972 and, following his death in a plane crash the next year, we wrote to the Queen and asked her permission to rename it Prince William School. Princess Alice gave us a beautiful photograph of Prince William which is hanging in the school today. I was chairman of the governors for ten years.

Reg Sutton

Walking or Cycling

I went to school in Titchmarsh and then in about 1930 I went to Thrapston. There was quite a bit of hullaballoo about it because we were told we either had to walk or cycle to Thrapston. So everyone was up in arms and we had taxis from Heighton's of Thrapston to take us. Later on we had buses. The school was in Market Road as it is now but in those days it was called Thrapston C of E School. There was another school at the top of Huntingdon Road that they called the Council School.

Raymond Gray

Fifteen More

There was a thing called Fifteen More. Breakfast was at a quarter to eight. At half past seven the youngest boy in the bottom dormitory shouted out 'fifteen more'. A minute later, another boy shouted out 'fourteen more' and so on so that the prefects knew how much longer they had to get up and shave.

The boys would have bacon and egg for breakfast but the main meal of the day was at lunchtime. There were plenty of suet puddings, I remember that! In the evening it was something like baked beans on toast.

For Sunday lunch there was a roast and it was the tradition that the housemaster carved. By the time you had carved for forty-three boys, the chap who had been served first would have a cold meal.

Alec Payne

By Train

When you were eleven you had to go to Oundle to school so we went on the train from Barnwell. We went to Milton Road School, which was the church school in Oundle.

Eileen Woolman

Trying to Keep Warm

After I was a house tutor in Sydney House I was appointed as housemaster of Crosby House where I spent fifteen years. Crosby was the last house to be 'modernized' as they called it in those days. The boys had a cold bath every morning, which was supervised by the prefects. In the dormitories there was a fireplace but for safety's sake it was never lit so in order to keep warm the boys put sheets of newspaper between the blankets.

There were four dorms with twelve to fourteen boys. There was always a prefect in each one. In my day there were not many studies; I think there were about eight and they were shared by three boys.

They boys had hip baths and when they got rid of them and we had proper plumbing installed, the boys took the baths and used

Barnwell School in 1930. From left to right, back row: Bernard Taylor, Dennis Beeby, Ernest Noble, Bernard Pepper, Harold Russell, Aubrey Russell. Middle row: Elsie George, Mary Marriott, Joyce Marriott, Kathleen Tough, Barbara George, Muriel Russell. Seated: Tommy Noble, Sidney Noble, Trevor Marriott, Stanley Peacock, Nora Marriott, Norah Marriott, Kenneth Russell.

them as coracles and paddled around in the open-air swimming bath!

Alec Payne

Two Norahs

I went to Barnwell School and we had a headmistress then who was called Miss Naish. My great friend was Nora Marriott. In a village this size there were two Norah Marriotts but she was no relation. Her father was chauffeur to the McGraths at Barnwell Manor. Kath Batley, who was Kathleen Tough in those days, was at school with me. When I started school I must have been five. We had big desks and Miss Naish used to

draw in chalk on them a big A or a big B and we had little sea shells and put them round this letter. Then we used to gradually get to chalking the letter ourselves and putting the shells round it. Looking back I wonder how we ever learnt our letters.

When we were little we sat two to a desk. The last year I was at Barnwell School, I was nine I suppose, and Mrs Dickinson came. We had reading books with stories in them. We had never had any reading books before. We had two piles of books in a great big cupboard. One was called 'Stories of Far Away Lands' and the other was 'People of Long Ago'. I always remember, we used to get these books out and we used to read and read them until you knew them off by heart. There were two things that always puzzled me: one was that the Ancient

Barnwell School and the schoolhouse, which outwardly have barely changed.

Britons painted their skins with woad that was blue. Nobody ever told me why they did it. But the thing that worried me more was the story about pygmies. Well, if they were pygmies, why weren't they like pigs? And they never had any clothes, according to the book. So did they have little tails like pigs? Nobody ever enlightened me about all this.

Norah Blunt

Foul Play

We used to play football in the street but if the bobby saw us he would pick the ball up and cut it.

Eric Jones

A New National School

When my grandfather came here there was a very strong Church of England side and the Dissenters side. My grandfather was a very strong Baptist, almost a Fundamental Baptist so he was determined that his children wouldn't go to the church school (which was the only school in Thrapston at the time) so he sent them to a little private school in Islip.

When the 1895 Education Act came out, it allowed schools to be run other than by the church. My grandfather was on the parish council and he got together with the headmaster of this private school in Islip and one or two others and they got the National School going. It started off in a little tin hut in Grove Road but in 1903 it

moved to a new building at the top of Huntingdon Road.

My grandfather was chairman of the governors ever since it was formed until his death in 1926. It became known as the 'top school' and the Church of England school, in Market Road, was called 'the back lane school'.

Philip Loaring

In 1936 there was a fire in Sydney House at Oundle School, supposedly caused by the airing of blankets in front of a fire by the matron.

Get Your Scarf

There was the chance for every boy to wear a scarf at Oundle School. If you were a first team rugger player, a cricketer, a second, a house colour – you had a particular scarf. That meant that at break times they were all wearing theses different scarves, having congregated at the Tuck Shop and eating their buns. If you were not a 'scarf' you

The passenger waiting room at Barnwell being moved for use with the Nene Valley Railway at Stibbington.

were a bit out of it. The school was dominated by the games players of those days.

Alec Payne

What's in a Name?

The Miss Parkers used to live where Mr Macadam lives now. It's called Parker's Patch now but I'm sure Miss Parker would never agree with that name. She always called it 'The Old Cottage'. The older Miss Parker, Miss Ethel Parker, was a schoolteacher and her younger sister, Constance, was, as you would say in those days, 'fragile'. Connie didn't do anything. I am sure she once taught at Barnwell but when I went to Oundle Council School she was teaching there. She used to cycle there every day.

I used to go on the train and we used to get in the back. The farther back you went, the longer ride you got. The entrance to the school was along South Road but we always went in off West Street.

Norah Blunt

Just to Prove it

Occasionally, but not very often, on the last night of the school term a boy would climb the steeple of Oundle church. In the morning you would find a chamber pot on top. It had to be stopped because they were risking life and limb.

We had school trains. They ran to Oundle station from either Peterborough or Northampton. When the boys left to go home, they often had to be at Oundle station by six thirty in the morning.

Alec Payne

CHAPTER 4
Working Life

John William Starsmore Snr, who was miller at Yarwell and also a Methodist Lay Preacher at Yarwell and Nassington.

Delivering Newspapers

I did forty-three years delivering newspapers and each day I travelled thirty-nine miles. I used to get the papers from Leayton's paper shop which is now Greens or Oundle News. Mr Leayton came in and said he wanted somebody to do the papers for one week. So I did it and he never seemed to get anybody else so I kept on with it. I started at seven in the morning at Barnwell Mill, went to all the huts along the Barnwell Road – where the garden centre is now – then up to Cuckoo Pen to deliver Mr Beesley's. Then I did all Barnwell and up Armston Road to Armston, then Thurning and on to Winwick and Hamerton. Then it was back from Hamerton to Steeple Gidding, Little Gidding, Great Gidding, Luddington and Hemington.

I had been doing it for a bit and then I bought the round. Sometimes I had to go to Peterborough to collect the papers but usually they dumped them in Oundle and I picked them up from there. I was driving a Standard.

Harold Ashby

Farm Work

When my mother was first pregnant it did-n't mean she could take life easily. She had to go on doing her work on the farm. She had her poultry to look after. They were impor-tant because the money that came in for the eggs and the chickens fed and clothed us. All the money my mother had to keep house was from her butter and the eggs and chickens. She raised fifteen to twenty geese for Christmas and they were taken to market in December.

Mary Thomson

Clicker and Closer

My father, Tom Pearson, was a foreman worker in the shoe factory and during the war they made army boots. He was a 'clicker' and my mother, Ethel, was a foreman or fore-woman 'closer'. A clicker assesses the skin and decides how many uppers they can cut out of the leather. A closer stitches the front and the back of the upper part of the shoe together. My mother would do a lot of sam-ples because she was so good at her job.

Jean Woodward

The Sack Factory

The Huntingdon race traffic used to come down the Huntingdon Road and they all converged at the corner of Oundle Road. The lorries didn't want to give way to one another on the bridge and there were no end of accidents.

Next to the garage on the Oundle Road was a factory they used to call the sack fac-tory. There were mostly girls employed there in the '50s. They made sacking and hessian and that sort of thing. After the sack factory closed, the shoe people took it over. They imported the shoes, repacked them and sent them out again.

There were quite a few little subsidiaries of shoe factories around Thrapston. They made uppers or soles for the bigger places in Irthlingborough and Northampton.

Eddie Rowe

Into Partnership

I came down from Yorkshire where I was born, with my parents and David my brother to Warmington. My father had taken on Tansor Grange Farm. When I started farm-ing myself, I went into partnership with John Vickers of Tansor Wold Farm and I took over

Ethel and Tom Pearson in the 1930s.

the farm when he left. When I first went there was a dairy but milking was a tie so we went out of cattle after about a year and we went into pigs. When Mr Vickers retired I carried on.

John Simpson

Little Jobs

When Harold delivered the papers he used to do all sorts of little jobs for people. He would fill up the buckets with water from outside and collect prescriptions.

Gladys Ashby

Forty-Seven Years

I went to school with Wilfred Osborne and we grew up together and we married. When he left school he went to work at Elton Hall in the gardens. He went there when he was fourteen and he finished when he was sixty-one.

Dorothy Osborne

Women's Work

We had a big dairy with around thirty milking cows. The womenfolk didn't milk but we had to do the washing and sterilising of the milk buckets and the filters. When I was a very little girl I remember when they made butter. We had a huge brown churn and you turned and turned the handle. And my mother, being a Devon woman, would always make clotted cream. It would take three days; you would take the milk – and it mustn't be

cooled – and you put it in a pancheon, which was a large shallow pan, and it was put in a cool place to set the cream. The next day you put it on the hob just so that it bubbled but you had to make sure it did not boil. And that makes a lovely crust. You put it back in a cool place in the cellar and on the third day you use a shallow skimmer and you have gorgeous thick cream. With the remaining milk my mother made lovely cakes or she fed the calves or the dog with it.

Mary Thomson

Repairing Bicycles

My grandfather started the garage in 1904. He had a shed beside his house. He started as a cycle business, mainly repairing them, in Newton Road on the corner of London Road. He used to sell paraffin and I remember as a child going into a barn at the side of the house and this petroly, oily smell! We were not really supposed to go in there.

Jean Woodward

Wooden Topped

In the shop there were all wooden topped tables. The butcher's blocks were made of Canadian maple because there were no knots in the wood. They were cut into blocks and set upright to the grain and then clamped round the outside. That meant that when you cut on it you were not cutting across the grain you were cutting into the top of the grain. We delivered to our customers by carrier bikes and two little Austin 7 vans to the villages.

Philip Brudenell

Pattern Maker

I started work at Smith & Grace. I was determined to be an engineer and in those days my clock number was 407. That was in the days when the population in Thrapston was just under 2,000. They were not all Thrapston people who worked there; they used to come from Denford, Islip, Titchmash and all over the place.

Smith & Grace manufactured pulleys and anything in cast iron. I went there as a pattern-maker apprentice and when the war came I was making things like handles to go in submarines and little wheels. There were special lathes for turning tank turrets. There was one woman, during the war, who worked two capstan lathes.

One day, Mr Brookfield called me in. 'There's a package for you, lad,' he said. 'Make some up and we'll get them cast.' I opened it up and inside was a Mills bomb. I took it into the workshop, sawed it in half, cleaned it all up, and eventually made some aluminium castings and then we used to turn out these Mills bombs.

Philip Loaring

Farm Work

When I left school I went to work for Harry Howel at Glebe Farm between Lowick and Sudborough and I did farm work. I worked for him for fifteen months and then went on to work for Joe Day at Alley Farm in Lowick. I did six months on a threshing contract and then twelve and a half years with Johnny Bosworth back in Islip.

I worked for the River Board for sixteen and a half years, cleaning weeds out of the River Nene and keeping the channels down and the brooks all clean and tidy through the winter. We worked from Ringstead down to Wadenhoe, that was our stretch. That was from 1964 to 1980. There were some long boats that used to come from Wisbech going to Northampton but they packed up because of the flooding. They couldn't get through the locks and they were losing time. Sometimes they were standing there more than three weeks before they could move.

John Jeffs

The Last Miller

I was born in Nassington and came to Yarwell in 1931. We had farmed the Mill Farm since 1906: first my grandfather, then my father and then myself. They were both named John William but they named me Jack.

I was the last miller at Yarwell Mill. We never lived there; we lived at Vine House. We ran the milling business and delivered corn and flour and cooking flour and pig meal around all the local villages by horse and cart.

The corn and flour was in 7 or 14lb paper bags and the pig meal was in hessian sacks. We took them around to Yarwell, Nassington and Apethorpe, Wansford, Thornhaugh, Upton, Sutton and Castor. We took pheasant food to Colonel Brassey on the Apethorpe Estate every Friday.

Farmers used to bring their corn to be milled on a Tuesday and collect it on a Friday. There were no other mills close by. Elton Mill was doing mostly estate work for Elton Hall. In 1943 we lost the miller who went on the railway to do a more specialised job so that left me on my own. But it didn't pay so I stopped working the mill.

Jack Starsmore

Yarwell Mill.

Grave Digging

I started grave digging in 1960 in Islip then after twelve year I started contracting it around. They use the same tools now as what I used – that's a pick, shovel, spade, fork. I come to Crowson's in Barnwell in 1980.

John Jeffs

Helping Out

I went to a secretarial college in South Molton Street, London and lived with my aunt in Streatham. Then my mother died after a year so I came back to Thrapston to look after dad and my sister and I went on to work in the shop.

Joyce Bird

Original Features

After I left school I was in the WAAF for two years and then I went to help mother in the shop. It has been bought now by Tasty Bites but they have left a lot of the original features like the mahogany shelving and the old counter. There is even a picture of my mother hanging over the till. In the garden at the back, there is a pump against the back wall which used to be in our scullery. We were rather surprised when they took up the kitchen floor and they found a well nearly in the middle.

Pru Goss

To Market

My father would go to market from Great Addington. Thrapston was his regular mar-

Jack Starsmore and his father, William ploughing at Yarwell.

ket. That was on Tuesdays and he always went there. He went in the pony and buggy until he had a car, which would be about 1925. It was a Humber. Sometimes we would go to Kettering market and mother would go to the shops there, and occasionally father would go to Northampton market, which was nineteen miles away – always in the pony and buggy.

Mary Thomson

Daisy

Our carthorse was Daisy and when she came back from Castor and Sutton, she got to the Great North Road and I'd guide her across and then I could throw the reins down in the cart and she'd find her way back to the mill. She would go right up to the mill door to take the empty sacks out before she was put away. We had her for over twenty years.

Jack Starsmore

Reviving the Market

There was no market through the war years and after the war, but because Oundle market rights go back to the sixteenth century a market could be set up at any time. Jimmy Norman's father had a market garden at Castor and they used to come over on a Thursday and put some bedding plants in boxes on the ground in the market place. The shop the Normans use now was a shoe shop – Blacks – and Jimmy and his father decided to set up there. Eventually, they were joined by other people and the town council promoted the market.

Philip Brudenell

Fire!

In 1921 at the beginning of June, I was nine, and Jean was a few days old and my mother was still in bed. I think it was usual to stay in bed for at least two weeks after the birth of a baby in those days. Someone in a cottage opposite saw a fire start in one of our hay ricks. They said it was started by petrol because the flame was blue. It was about midnight on a Saturday. At that time the Sinn Fein were setting fire to stack yards every weekend all across the country. I can well remember my auntie Margaret and I going up to the attic and looking out at all these fires. It was very frightening.

There was a stream by the gate that never dried up and there was a string of villagers from the stream right up to the stack yard and they had buckets they filled from the stream and passed from hand to hand. It didn't do much good. The fire brigade arrived, and this was a small fire engine pulled by two galloping horses. They put the fire out eventually but all the ricks were destroyed. Fortunately, the wind that was blowing over the house changed direction so the fire didn't reach the house. The dog that was chained up in the yard was saved but my mother's chickens all died. It took several hours before they got it under control.

I remember going out the next morning with my father and I can still smell the terrible smell of burnt hay and burnt buildings and equipment.

Mary Thomson

Local Deliveries

We were milking twenty Friesian cows each day and delivering milk in Nassington and Yarwell. We used a pony and trap to deliver in those days and the milk was put in ten and fifteen gallon churns. Then we changed to a motor car with the front seat out. When we arrived with the milk, people had their jugs or cans ready for us to fill.

Jack Starsmore

Jack Starsmore's father, William, with one of the fine horses he used to show.

The Molecatchers

In Barnwell I remember two Molecatchers. One was Harold Kisby and the other was George Hipwell. Mr Kisby lived next door to where Dora Robinson used to live and Mr Hipwell lived in one of the cottages that were burnt down in the village. That was about 1920 and they said a spark from the train set fire to the two houses at the top of the lane and sparks from that went to the next houses, so four cottages were burnt down.

Eileen Woolman

A Long Haul

We delivered to the Rothchilds at Ashton Wold and usually I went up there on my bike. If the cook didn't like what I had I had to take it back. When I got back to the shop they would have had a phone call to say I was bringing the meat back and so I would have to take some more to them. It's a long haul by bike up to Ashton Wold – at least three miles and there are hills.

Philip Brudenell

Skinning a Rabbit

When my mother used to skin a rabbit she used to have a stick that she put down the centre to stretch it longways. When you cut off the head you put it in the neck. Then she put another stick crosswise which went between the front legs. Then it could be laid out to dry. When they were dry she sold them. They used the skins to make fur collars and fur gloves and so on.

Mary Thomson

Moving Round

I worked for Siddons the coal merchants in Oundle for about thirteen years. I worked in the office which is now the delicatessen shop. North & Perkins who sold foodstuffs for poultry and that sort of thing also belonged to Siddons & Sons. They were on the opposite side of the road. I used to ride a bicycle from Barnwell and I'd go home for dinner!

Walter was a policeman in Oundle. We married in 1937 and I left Barnwell and we moved to Kettering and then Northampton and from there to West Haddon and out to Middleton Cheney. We went round the county. We came back here to Barnwell in 1957 after Walter retired.

Eileen Woolman

Markets

In between the wars, Oundle and Thrapston both had viable cattle markets. Oundle's cattle market was down Pick Arthy's and it was taken over by Burgesses who sold lawnmowers and agricultural equipment. Southam's ran Oundle market and Bletsoe's ran Thrapston market.

Philip Brudenell

My First Job

My first job was working at Oundle Motors which is now Pick Arthy's. First of all I served the petrol because I was only fifteen but then I went to work in the offices and it was a very good job. It was owned in those days by Mr Salsbury and I left when Geoff Willimont bought it. He came and asked me to go back and I did for short periods and then gradually for a longer time.

Audrey Knight

A Job I Hated

I left school to look after my mother who was ill. When she got better my father said he thought it was time I got a job. I went to the employment bureau and they told me about this job at the tax office in Wellingborough. My father thought it sounded all right so I went for an interview and got the job. I hated every minute of it! I wanted to be either a hairdresser or a journalist. Several of my friends from school were already working there.

I started off as a P3 Clerk which meant being a dog's body – doing the filing, making the tea, that sort of thing. You didn't call anybody by their Christian name, ever. Even the girls I had been at school with I had to call Miss Smith or Miss Hall. I wasn't allowed to call them Doreen and Valerie as I had for the previous five years. It was very formal. There was not really a dress code but you never wore trousers and I never went without tights, even in the hottest summer.

To get promotion you had to pass exams. From P3 you went to be a Clerical Assistant, and then you went on to be a Tax Officer. I think it took me about a year to become a Tax Officer which meant I was then eligible for a marriage allowance or a pension. After six years you could take your marriage allowance which I did in lieu of a pension. By this time I had married John Darnell so I claimed the £50 and we used it to go to Paris!

Jean Woodward

Poultry

My father, mother and brother moved to Islip from Wellingborough in 1916. They rented the house because it had some land. My father was interested in poultry and after he sold the hardware business he went into poultry. He put in incubators, and he hatched and despatched chickens all over the country. They were sent by rail from Thrapston station and then the business developed into poultry fattening and he rented more land. The chickens were prepared and trussed and taken to Smithfield market every day. A haulier from Market Deeping would meet us at Peterborough each night to take the poultry to London.

Phyllis Whittaker

Ruining the Land

My father was no horseman and although he didn't forbid the hunt to come across the land, he didn't like it because the horses cut up the grass and made a mess of the land sometimes. It was the Woodland Pytchley Hunt and the hounds were kennelled at Pipewell. The Oakleigh used to come once or twice a season. As far as I remember there were no fox coverts on our land.

Mary Thomson

Spraying the Crops

I was one of the people who revolutionised agriculture. I was working for a firm called Pest Control. Between the war years agriculture in this country was allowed to go down the drain. Most land was put down to pasture because we could import food cheaper than it could be grown here. When the Second World War came, there was pasture to grow crops but the war lasted longer than expected and after three years we were in very serious trouble. Farming that had been based on a rotational system was scrapped and we went in for monoculture for food. In 1945 there was the 'weed and pest population explosion' because we had packed up our traditional methods. My boss, Dr Ripper, was a German Jew, and he came over to this country as an entomologist and set up a small crop-spraying company.

We had no machinery but during the war years we managed to mackle things up. When I joined the company I designed some of the machines but I became a crop sprayer and my job was to control weeds and pests using chemicals. We used big spraying machines and I sprayed farms right down as far as Northampton and up as far as Stamford. We used American bean sprayers, which held 500 gallons of spray and the application rate was 100 gallons an acre. Going up the steep hills we couldn't use wheel tractors so I got the crawler tractors. We had four or five teams that used to operate in the Nene valley and the Welland valley. The spraying machines worked night and day. These big spraying machines used 1,000 gallons of water every hour. We got it from the streams and rivers.

As the chemicals changed, we didn't need these big machines because farmers could put the spray on the back of a tractor.

When we used to go to the Oundle area to spray we would stay at The Rose and Crown.

George Pickworth

Regular Use

We used the station almost daily. We used to have goods delivered by rail from Tuxford & Tebbitt who were pie manufacturers in Melton Mowbray. That was in rationing times. The pies would arrive in wooden boxes wrapped in straw.

Before there was refrigeration, we had blocks of ice that came by rail from Peterborough where there was an ice factory. When they arrived at Oundle station, they were brought up to the shop and put in the cold room. It would stay there until it melted. In my time, we had a refrigeration box built that was six feet square and it had a compressor that sent cold air around. It was replaced soon after the war with a modern refrigeration unit.

Philip Brudenell

Eggs, Please!

The railway ran along the edge of Mill Farm and the engine driver used to signal to the mill when he wanted eggs. When the one o'clock train came down, if it whistled as he passed, it meant he wanted his three dozen eggs. It was a fixed order and granddad would take them to Nassington station for the twenty past four train when he was on the way back.

Jack Starsmore

Walking the Cattle

When I married Vincent Whittaker I went to live at Grange Farm in Slipton. When they moved from Teeton near

Northampton to Slipton, they walked the cattle across. That is about twenty miles. In my mother's family, one brother farmed at a lodge farm and the other farmed in Slipton, which is how Vin and I met. I was thirty-nine when we married. Vin had an invalid father and I had an invalid mother. I worked in the telephone exchange, which was on the corner of Market Road in Thrapston, but I gave that up to look after my mother. I started there on 25 April 1935 as a part-time telephonist.

Phyllis Whittaker

Making Changes

I came to Oundle in 1951 to modernise the telephone exchange system. It was a manual exchange in those days, with three girl operators who sat in a room above the post office counter. We installed a new telephone exchange in Drumming Well Lane. The building there was put up in 1946 but the post office couldn't afford to put in the new apparatus at that time. This new exchange dealt with calls not only from Oundle but from the exchanges at Winwick, Benefield and Cotterstock. They were all worked into Oundle and from Oundle to Peterborough. There was an operator to answer at Peterborough if necessary.

It took from the beginning of 1951 until Tuesday 11 December 1951 to complete when it changed over from manual to automatic at one thirty in the afternoon. That was used until the 1970s when a new exchange was put in but I had retired by then.

Reg Sutton

The Dairy

Sid Rowell was a dairy farmer and he had his dairy at the bottom of Stoke Hill and a shop on the corner of Mill Road and Stoke Hill where you could buy cream and butter.

Philip Brudenell

One of the Best

Thrapston Market is one of the best markets in the area. I should say it is one of the best in East Anglia. There are often a lot of smells here on market day when they wash out because some of the water goes down the old sewerage system. If you are outside Barclays Bank you get the smells coming up. There was talk of moving the market, maybe up to the industrial estate but they haven't got around to that.

Eddie Rowe

Not Months but Years

After I left school I went into the business with my father for about eighteenth months and then I did my national service after which I went back. I didn't want to do butchery particularly because I was more mechanically minded. I expected to help out for a few months but that turned into forty years!

Philip Brudenell

From Trailer to Three Lorries

We ran a livestock haulage business for twenty-nine years and we closed that around 1980. We took stock to local markets and

Oundle Urban District Council in 1974. From left to right, back row: David Wills, Andrew Spurrell, John Booth, John Shingles, Jim Wild, Bernard Seaman (town clerk), -?-, Archie Marshall, Bob Cheney. Front row: Bill Peasgood, Ben Rowbotham, Reg Sutton (chairman), Albert Lane, ? Fleming. Standing in the centre are Mrs Cockin and Lottie Mason.

horses to Newmarket or we moved them for the hunt. We began by taking local villagers' pigs to market using a trailer behind the car. That was mainly to Stamford, Peterborough, Oundle and Thrapston markets. We went from a car and trailer to a lorry and then we got to three lorries. Sometimes we'd not get home until midnight and then there would be a dirty lorry to wash out.

Jack Starsmore

Council Work

My father went on to Oundle Town Council in the late fifties and in 1960 he was the chairman of the Council. I didn't go on the Council until 1985 and I had retired. In May 1986 I was elected to East Northamptonshire District Council. Just before I joined the Council, the Town Clerk was employed for two evenings a week. Now it has moved on with the increase of population and the management of the councils assets which all needs a lot of work. Now there is a full time Town Clerk and Deputy Clerk and a part time receptionist and secretary. This is not because of created work: it was mainly because things were not getting done.

Philip Brudenell

Tagging Along

I came into practice in Oundle with Freddie Smith. You tagged along in the same old way that everyone did in those days. My furthest calls were at Deeping St James, Spaldwick, Stanion, Little Oakley and we used to go out as far as Bury, the other side of Ramsey. If you look at the statistics of East Northants District, there are 125,000 acres and about ten years ago a population of 63,000, making roughly one person to two acres. We are in middle England here.

When I first started as a vet, our surgery was in Jericho. We moved out of there in November 1981 to come here in South Road so we have been here for nearly twenty years. I was due to qualify on 9 August 1962 but because this area had not been eradicated of TB in cattle, they were desperate to get on with the testing. Normally you had to be in practice for six months before you could become a local veterinary inspector, but because I lived here and I knew the area fairly well, I could become one immediately. There was not a lot of TB around here but we were one of the last areas to be cleared.

The problem was that during the war, refugees came over here and started drinking our milk and got TB. We had been drinking unpasteurised milk all our lives and built up an immunity, but the refugees who lived in the cities had only had pasteurised milk and so hadn't any immunity.

Andrew Spurrell

Early Start

We did mixed farming. There were three of us working men and we had cattle, sheep, pigs and poultry. There was arable as well. We farmed with horses when I was small and we had our first tractor in 1948. We changed it for a better one every five years.

We used to start at half past six in the morning. When I joined the farm after I left school there was no mains water. I used to have to go round to the water tanks and pump them full of water. There were four or five of these tanks around the farm. We had to fill them every day. There was a well and pump in the grass field in front of the house. When mains water was brought to the farm we filled in the well.

All the water tanks were connected. There was a pump in the end of the crew yard where there was a brick built water tank. There was also a pump in one of the cow places. When we didn't have any rain we ran out of water so I would go to the kitchen in Tansor Grange, get a cycle inner tube and attach it to the tap in there and hang that out of the window into the water cart. I still have part of that water cart.

John Preston

Threshers

I was born in Bozeat but I left there after a few months and I lived at Wollaston for eighty years and then I moved to Woodford. I was the eldest of ten and my father had a share in a small farm but I lived with my grandma from time to time. On the farm we had our own threshing machine and we used to go from farm to farm to thresh the corn. We probably went to twelve or fourteen farms in the area. It wasn't easy because the roads were very dirty and with potholes. These machines were very big and the moved very slowly. We moved them with a traction engine. This was the main income from our farm.

There were about ten or twelve men who worked on the machine. One was on the engine, one looking after the corn as it comes down the drum, one feeding the barn part, another looking after the chaff. There were a lot of jobs.

Eric Jones

River Traffic

Mainly the barges from the Nene Barge & Lighter Company at Wansford used to come up the river past the mill at Yarwell. They carried stone from the quarries and they would take it up the river to where it was required on the river bank for building the banks up.

Jack Starsmore

Earning a Bit

As I grew up I wanted to earn a bit of money so I went around with the milk cart. A friend had a dairy and I went round with him with a measure on a hook and put the milk in the jugs. Every morning about seven o'clock you had to harness the nag and get over to the farm where they milked about forty cows. We had two churns on the milk cart. One had ordinary milk and the other had skim. That was cheaper.

I did that for about two years until I got to be thirteen. I got permission from the school authorities to report at a quarter to ten in the morning instead of nine o'clock because I was helping with the milk. Then,

Philip Preston in the 16-acre field at Tansor Lodge Farm, that is towards Lutton and known then as Town Ground.

after school in the late autumn and winter, I'd harness the nag up, put him in the trap that used to hold four or five people. I would pick up people at their homes and drop them at the farm.

Eric Jones

Churning Butter

Farming was hard, physical work that had to be done day after day. We had cows but we didn't sell the milk. They used to make large quantities of butter and sell that. Granny Preston used to make 90lbs of butter a week. She used to go off on the bus to Oundle with a big wicker basket filled up three times a week to sell the butter. Amps used to take a lot of butter.

She made the butter in a big wooden churn. It was turning and turning and turning the handle. Sometimes she made it very quickly and sometimes it would take her two hours. It depended on the state of the milk. If you have a freshly calved cow the quality was very good and it made butter quickly.

John Preston

Selling at Thrapston Market

My mother used to make butter. We used to help churn the milk and there was a long wooden thing like a trough that had a wooden handle that you turned and it wound round and pressed all the moisture out. She used to take it to sell at Thrapston market on a Tuesday.

Norah Blunt

Fattening Pigs

We used to keep a lot of pigs and as when the sows farrowed there were eight or ten piglets. I didn't have a grandfather so Grandma was the boss of the farm. She used to look after the pigs and we'd take them away from the sow at six to eight weeks. They used to get really fat in those days. We fed them with a bit of pollard in the water and when the piglets were parted from the sows we put more in and the food got thicker. And as they got bigger, the food got thicker with water and pollard and barley flour and it was as much as you could do to stir it round. We always kept one for the local butcher which was shared around.

Eric Jones

Walking to Market

We walked the stock to market in Oundle. During the war you didn't sell by auction, the market was just a collecting centre and animals were paid on the grade. There was a local farmer, a local butcher and an auctioneer would handle every animal and decide on the quality of it. It was either super special, special, A plus or A minus and so on. When the controls came off in the 1950s, they kept Oundle market as an auction market but Thrapston had a very good market and took the trade. The whole of the site of the cattle market at Oundle was offered to Geoffrey Willimont for £3,000. We took our cattle then to Stamford market.

We got friendly with a butcher from Nassington, Jack Mould. He would come on the farm and pick the animals he wanted and arrange for them to be slaughtered in the slaughterhouse in the middle of the village.

Trevor Marriott sitting on the tractor pulling the grass cutter at Lower Farm in Barnwell.

The field at Tansor Lodge Farm that was right next to the crew yard was known as Home Close. And there was the second Home Close. If you go beyond the stockyard there was the forty-acre that was originally three fields so there was Top Field, Middle Field and Bottom Field.

We used to have an early breakfast about six in the morning. We came in again at nine o'clock for what we used to call lunch, then in again at twelve o'clock for dinner and then at five o'clock for tea and very often you would be out again and not in until nine or ten o'clock at night.

John Preston

Mining

They were building a military camp between here and Thrapston and I worked there for three months as a labourer when I recovered from TB and then I went to work at Islip blast furnaces. You used to get all the iron ore from Twywell and Lowick and Sudborough. There were drift mines there and I had to go down them once. They went all under Drayton Park. They used to bring the iron ore up in the narrow gauge railway and take it to the Islip furnaces.

They used to get the limestone along the turn that you used to go to Finedon, along the Kettering Road near Woodford.

I was a wagon inspector and I had to go around and see if the wagons had the cotter pins in and the bearings were all right. During the war they decided the furnaces would close down so we were then sent to Peterborough. We went on a special train there and we were interviewed to work on the railway. They thought the railways would be loaded with wounded and so there would have to be more trains and people to work on them. I was only there for three weeks and I had to go up to Nottingham for a medical and because I had had Tuberculosis they wouldn't take me on.

Then I went to Molesworth aerodrome

helping with maintenance. At that time the Americans were there. I was there when the King and Queen came and Princess Elizabeth. It was a big to-do then.

I went to work for a local builder, Mr Harold Turner after I left Molesworth. I had never done anything to do with building before but I worked for him for twenty-nine and a half years. At first it was Turner & Spendlove and they built the new council houses near the church in Titchmarsh. They parted company eventually and Mr Turner carried on until he ceased trading in 1976. I went to work for Keith Wright at Islip until I retired. I stopped work on my birthday on 8 February 1985.

Raymond Gray

David Jackson working the horse and binder, cutting corn and tying into sheaves. Seated are Tim, John and Ted Preston. (1938-1939).

Near the bottom green in Titchmarsh before 1914. On the left is the bakehouse.

Percy Marriott with his milk cart.

CHAPTER 5
People and Places

The wedding of Philip and Mary Preston in 1902 at Tansor.

The Circus

Roberts Brothers used to over-winter their circus animals at Polebrook for many years. When they came first, the railway was still going and a lot of the elephants used to come by rail and walk from the station to Polebrook.

Philip Brudenell

Shopkeepers in Oundle

Percy Amps was a bit of a character. He was a big, robust man who was a churchwarden and he often used to go to sleep in church. He would come out in his shorts, which were cut-off trousers. If you went into his shop and he was serving you, he would stop if someone like Lady Ethel Wickham came in and abandon you to serve her! I remember going upstairs one day, because we used to play with

Michael and Lawrence Amps, and Percy Amps was laying flat out on the settee and fanning himself. He never spoke to us.

Granny Selby had the ironmonger's shop where Jumpers is now. It was a really old-fashioned place with lots of little drawers for nails and screws. We would go over there when we were children. There was a big kitchen with a table in the middle. Sometimes she would go outside, down some steps and she would pick us grapes.

Granny Selby was very kind. She was small and she used to wear long black skirts. Her assistant was Olive Gilby. We used to call her Paraffin Liz when we were children because she always smelled of paraffin.

Ann Cheney

Farming Jockeys

My mother, Marjorie, was born in Fotheringhay. Her maiden name was Cheney and her father was a gentleman farmer who lived at Manor Farm. He rode in the Grand National twice, in 1904 and 1908, once on Trueville when he came 4th and then on Reliance when he came 8th. He went round Aintree seventeen times without coming off and his brother went round fifteen times. His brother used to farm at Luddington.

Andrew Spurrell

Where They Lived

The old estate yard belonging to the Manor became No. 8 Barnwell and my dad used to talk about Mr Maddison living there. He was the estate carpenter and it was also the estate

Reg Sutton and Philip Brudenell – president of Oundle Rotary – in 1975 with Tom Cunnington in a wheelchair presented to Oundle Care Committee.

manager's house. My granddad lived in Rose Cottage the other side of the Reading Room where Mr Vinson used to live. I lived there with Aunt Liz and Grandma Marriott for six months after Trevor was born and mother was in hospital.

When Trevor and Mary got married, they wanted to go and live there but father said they couldn't because it was too far from Lower Farm.

After I got married, I wanted to buy No. 31 Barnwell up that end, but father said I couldn't have it because I couldn't afford it! How did he know! Anyway, he said, he didn't want to sell it because he wanted it for a farm worker. Two months later he sold it to Harry Pike!

Norah Blunt

A photograph taken in Oundle in 1952, An unknown Oundle event, 1952. From left to right, back row: Tom Cunnington, Jack Horsford and Percy Amps. Front row: Lottie Mason, Mrs Cartwright, The Revd Cartwright and possibly, Miss Lloyd.

Marjorie Spurrell with one of her prize chihuahuas.

Youngest of Ten

When my parents married, my grandfather, Samuel Lawrence, was farming at Hemington. It was Hemington House Farm. He was a tall man, six foot, with brilliant blue eyes even when he was elderly. His hair was very curly and when I knew him it was white. He was always very smartly dressed in grey suits, with a waistcoat. He wore stiff collars and a cravat with a tie pin. He always had a handkerchief in his top pocket to match.

My grandfather was the youngest of seven farming sons and so he always had a rented farm. When he was a boy of ten, so the story goes, he saw a French clock with a pretty little dial and a gilt figure of a man. He bought it and took it home. When his father saw it he was so angry! My grandfather took it down to the housekeeper's cottage and she kept it for him in a cardboard box in her spare bedroom. That was the start of his collecting.

He collected all his life – clocks, furniture, porcelain. He would often go to an auction or a bankrupt sale and buy everything! My poor grandmother! The farm he had in Hemington was owned by the Duke of Buccleugh and my grandfather wrote to him explaining he had a great collection of porcelain and could he have an extra room built on to the farmhouse. The Duke came to see him and was so impressed to see his collection, which included two great Sevres vases, and agreed to build on a room.

When he left the farm it was taken over by Ben Measures.

Mary Thomson

Bobby Letch

There was an old chap who used to lodge in a thatched cottage on the right hand side of the road and he used to fetch the papers in a horse and cart. His name was Bobby Letch, a funny old chap with a beard. He used to collect the papers from Thorpe station. It was a high cart that you could put things in.

Raymond Gray

Interest Free and a Couple of Paintings

In 1963 I put an advert in *Exchange & Mart* saying, 'Writer wants to rent very cheap rural cottage' and received a reply about a small cot-

On Maundy Thursday it was usual to distribute bread to needy families in Oundle. Pictured outside the parish church are, from left to right, Revd Cartwright, Mr and Mrs Markham and Audrey Hooton (now Knight), during the 1940s.

tage for sale in Barnwell. The asking price was £400. I hadn't got £400 but it seemed so cheap, I couldn't resist taking a day off to investigate. I rejected the very small, rot-smelling cottage, sandwiched in a row of three as I peered through the letterbox. The neighbours who kept the key were out so I couldn't get inside. But the sun on the bright willows, the old bridge and the brook made me want a further look and two weeks later, the keys of No. 22 Barnwell were mine. The owner, who didn't live in the village, proposed the most generous terms of payment: £200 down, £150 paid off interest free at £2 a week and two small paintings by my husband, Frank Bowling.

Paddy Kitchen

Quaint

In the 1950s, Thrapston was a quaint town. There were two hotels – The White Hart and The Swan – and several pubs. The White Hart was just before you turn into Chancery Lane from the main street. It was an old coaching inn and you could see in the yard where the horses were tied up and the stage-coach was kept. Part of the gateway is still there. The Swan stood where the fire station is now. There was also The Bull's Head and The Red Lion but they have gone.

Eddie Rowe

Hidden Assets

Eric and Agnes Garratt lived next door to me at No. 21 Barnwell. Eric told me once that the reason the tap in my house, No. 22, was four inches from the ground and hidden under the stairs was because when water was piped to the village, Florence Swingler, who last lived in the cottage, was so afraid people would steal hers, she insisted the tap was placed out of sight of

Church elders at the last service in the Congregational Church in Oundle, now the Stahl Theatre,

Chairman of Oundle Urban District Council, Edgar Brudenell, in 1960 signing the 1000th account at the Trustee Savings Bank when it was in New Street, Oundle.

the window. In those days, used water had to be emptied away in the yard outside, from where it drained straight into the brook.

Eric looked like a weathered garden gnome but with a pair of the neatest, most dapper feet I had seen.

Paddy Kitchen

Tinker Booth

There was a chap here in Thrapston called Tinker Booth. He had retired when I came to Thrapston but I used to talk to him. He was a tinsmith by trade and he lived in a little cottage at the end of Dillon's shop. He had a little workshop there and used to make tin mugs and pots and that sort of thing.

When Jack Green bought the shop he incorporated the cottage into it.

Before I came here he used to help the undertaker and he used to bring the bodies up to the cemetery on a handcart.

He was a smart man, quite tall – about five foot nine or ten – with a bit of a stubble of beard, and he used to wear a flat cap.

Eddie Rowe

Button Horn

Button Horn was a postman but he had a smallholding and he kept geese. He was very well-known in the town.

Philip Brudenell

73

One-bedroom Houses

There was something going on at the chapel in Elton almost every night. We had Bible study on a Monday night, Tuesdays was for a Guild meeting and I think there was a junior guild but I can't remember which night that was. Then there was the girl's league and Friday night was choir practice.

There used to be lots of one-bedroom houses in Elton. There were rows of them and they were either knocked down or two or three were made into one house. The village has changed. Sir Richard Proby lived at Berryleas when he was first married and where the Briggs live was the old coach house.

Dorothy Osborne

Lottie Mason was well known in the area. She lived in Benefield Road and then moved to Danford Close. At one time she was chairman of Oundle Urban District Council.

Charlie and George ...

There were two men in the late forties called Charlie and George who lived at the Union, which was on Glapthorn road where Stronglands is now. It was the old workhouse and a stone building. It was called the Union but it was nicknamed the Spike. George and Charlie were both dwarfs and their feet were deformed. They had a handcart and they used to come into town and do shopping for various people at the Union. When it was time to go back, Charlie was usually rather tired so George would put him in the hand-cart and wheel him home.

Philip Brudenell

... or Snitch and Snatch

There were two little old boys we called Snitch and Snatch and they were only about four foot nine and they lived in the work-house. The Glapthorn Road Hospital was the workhouse and when the name was changed to the Glapthorn Road Hospital in 1948, father lined us all up and said, whatever you do you are not allowed to call it the workhouse. Don't you dare ever call it the workhouse again!

Andrew Spurrell

Dora Robinson

Dora left Barnwell School at fourteen and went to live with an aunt who ran the post office in Cotterstock. She used to deliver telegrams to Tansor, Fotheringhay and Southwick by bicycle.

Then she came back to Barnwell and

A group or Oundle councillors at an unknown event with Cllr Bennett (second right), Cllr North, Lottie Mason (centre) with Marjorie Spurrell and third from the left, Alec Wright, the rating officer who also ran the cinema.

A gathering of clergy at Oundle vicarage. On the right is Mr Markham and the bishop (with the crook) is Bishop Blagden, at one time Bishop of Peterborough.

Entrance to the old workhouse in Oundle. The police station now stands on the right.

worked at the rectory before becoming fourth housemaid at the Manor.

Paddy Kitchen

Bob Butt

Bob Butt was the engineer at Oundle School when they generated their own electricity. They were not on the national grid and in Blackpot Lane where the workshops are now, was the engine room. There was a great big generator and Bob Butt's job was to look after that. He had another sideline: when there was a fire it was his job to set off the maroons. You could hear them all over the town and they would alert the firemen who would race to the fire station. He did that as a part-time job.

Bob was a great romancer and he would tell the most incredible stories. One of his stories was about the First World War. In that war, Bob was a serving soldier and prior to that he had worked at Oundle School. He was captured by the Germans and one day, all the prisoners were lined up and there was a German general inspecting them. When he got to Bob he said, 'Bob? You must be Bob Butt!' The German general had been educated at Oundle School!

Another story he told was how one day he saw some wild duck flying overhead. He raced in the house, grabbed his gun but because he didn't have time to go back outside he aimed up the chimney and killed both birds!

There are other stories about Bob and if they were all collected they would fill a book!

Philip Brudenell

Watercress Harry

Watercress Harry used to come here. He used to go around Thrapston selling little bunches of watercress for 2d. Some of the ladies used to give him his dinner. They would leave it out on the wall and he would come along and eat it and leave a couple of bunches of watercress to pay for it. He had a beard and looked like an old seaman. I think he slept rough.

Eddie Rowe

Delivering Milk

Mr Rowell used to come round with his horse and trailer, and Mr Ray used to come round and fill up the jugs that were put out on the doorstep with milk. George Ray always used to wear britches and leather gaiters.

Andrew Spurrell

Agnes Broome

Miss Broome lived in a bungalow near the end of the village and her father was once the stationmaster in Barnwell. She told me she used to lodge with the Crowsons when she worked in Oundle during the war, and in the evenings, because she had nothing better to do, she used to help paint the carts and wagons. In those days, Crowson's was more of a wheelwright's than an undertaker's. As wheelwrighting died out, so Mr Crowson took up decorating and he took on Arthur Malster as a boy.

Paddy Kitchen

Bicycles

Vinco bicycles were made here in Elton. That's why we have Vinco terrace. Then it moved to the bottom of the school lane and eventually to Heighton's garage.

Dorothy Osborne

Dick Catlin

Dick Catlin was Welsh. Jean, my wife, worked for Southam's, the auctioneers, and Dick and I used to go and set out property for sale. Dick kept pigs and he used to take them to Kettering market using a pony, called Ginger, and a cart. He used to hold up all the traffic in Thrapston. Once Dick and I picked up a piano in the cart. We'd had a drink and we stopped outside Dick's house because he wanted to go inside for something. Now, when you tied Ginger up he would stand there all day but as soon as you got in the cart and let the reins go loose, he'd shoot off. Well, we hadn't put the pins properly in the tailgate of the cart and when we set off again the piano shot off the back! It stayed upright and slid down the street. Sergeant Pell and one of the Constables were looking out of the police station window and saw this happen. We had to go in the Beehive and get the lads out of the pub to help us get it back in and then we took it up to Bythorn. A couple of days later Sergeant Pell saw us and said: ' I've seen *Steptoe and Son* on the television but I've never seen anyone like you pair!'

Dick was a shortish man who wore a flat cap and liked a drink. His wife used to bawl her head off. When Dick and his wife fell out there was a commotion! She was a Yorkshire woman and had a voice like a pair of bellows! She didn't choose her words very well, either!

Walter G Brown was the first auctioneer in Thrapston when I came here and Jean worked for him. He was an estate agent as well.

Eddie Rowe

Waste Paper

Waste paper or salvage used to be collected in the Market Place where the Norwich and Peterborough Building Society is now.

Ann Cheney

Alec and Val

Alec Manning came from Denford and Val Drain kept a shop here. They used to take the train to Hunstanton and if it was late, they would get off the train before it got to

Gas containers weaving through the narrow North Street in Oundle en route to Bacton, north of the river Thames, well before the bypass was built.

its destination so they could get a beer at 12 o'clock.

Alec used to make lovely home made bread and he used to come round the pubs on a Saturday night selling it. He had a great big basket full of loaves and he used to come round, always smoking his pipe. He was always humming when he came round the pubs.

Eddie Rowe

Tony Evans

It is not that long ago that Tony Evans used to sweep the streets of Oundle. He was so conscientious he would even pick up rubbish on his way home and put it in his pocket to put in his dustbin. He always had a word for everyone but if you wanted to talk to him you had to walk along side him because he wouldn't stop working.

Philip Brudenell

The Pubs

In Warmington we had The Anchor, The Hautboy and Fiddle and the Red Lion. That is only three pubs but Titchmarsh had fourteen. Tansor had two.

John Simpson

A Fine – or Wet – Day Walker

Lady Ethel Wickham kept Jersey cows for milk and from time to time when she had a calf she didn't know what to do with, we would buy it.

Even if it was a pouring wet day, she would go for walks. She would walk around this way from Cotterstock, through Tansor and straight across the cross roads that were there before they altered the road. She would turn right as if she was going to Ashton and then right again and come along the bridle path to Tansor Lodge. One Saturday afternoon, it was raining like mad, but she had noticed on her walk that we had some Christmas Roses in the front bed. She couldn't grow them so she asked could she beg one?

John Preston

C.A.B. Marshall

'Cabby' Marshall or Arthur Marshall, who was housemaster of New House before becoming a famous face on television in a quiz show called *Call my Bluff*, introduced 'Masterpieces'. He had acted from time to time during the war. On the last night of the winter term he made all the staff appear on stage and do something. In my first year I was wrapped up in a huge overcoat and had to do something and finally they wrapped a scarf around my head and off I went. On the last performance, the headmaster came on in my overcoat with the scarf round his head. Everyone thought it was me until they took it off to reveal the headmaster!

I also appeared singing a duet with Ian Hepburn. I really hadn't got a voice but we had to sing 'Knock 'em in the Old Kent Road'.

Alec Payne

Lady Ethel

Church Farm, Cotterstock was owned by Lady Ethel Wickham of Cotterstock Hall and when I applied to take it over she wanted to see me. I went to see her and after that I had tea with her every fortnight. She came out with all sort of tales. She used to go hunting at Melton Mowbray and Ken Dunham's father took a horse there for her. She galloped over in her pony and trap, went hunting for the day, and the horse was brought back afterwards.

Lady Ethel was a very formidable woman. She was always very active; I remember going shooting with her when she was eighty-four. She swore like a trooper, too. I knew her in the 1960s.

John Simpson

Ginger

Percy Thompson, a vet who qualified in 1909, was known as Ginger to his friends. He had this double-fronted house in West Street. The vet before him was Sunny Nichols but he was probably just a horse doctor. Freddie Smith joined Captain Thompson (he had fought in the Boer War) in 1943.

Andrew Spurrell

Always Doing Something

My mother was always a restless woman and she couldn't bear to be alone. I remember her ringing Jessica up and saying, 'Could you come and do a jigsaw puzzle with me at 3.40 until 4 o'clock because I am not doing anything in that twenty minutes. Sometimes if you were walking down the street she would knock on the window and ask you in to have coffee. I knew there were some people, even those who were friends of hers, who would creep past under the window so she wouldn't see them and drag them in! She used to have masses of chihuahuas.

She was a professional skater. She began by training to be a Norland Nurse and then she came back and she used to ride a motorbike. She met a lady called Peggy Skinner and they both went skating and they started to teach it at Oxford. In the Wembley Exhibition of 1928, they gave demonstrations. They had a round thing that they froze and gave demonstrations on that.

Andrew Spurrell

Friar's Close Farm

There was a poultry farm over at Friar's Close long before Cook's had a turkey farm there. It must have started in 1934 because we celebrated the Silver Jubilee of King George V and Queen Mary up there. It must have closed in 1938 because we celebrated the coronation of King George VI up there. They reared hatched chickens there until they were so many weeks old and then they were killed and plucked and crated ready to send to the International Stores.

There was a hostel for about fifty men and fifty women. We used to have all these 'do's' in the recreation hall.

Norah Blunt

The Barnwell Roosters

In the 1930, Friar's Close Farm was still part of Barnwell Castle Estate, then owned by Major Colin Cooper. He initiated an ambitious chicken farm there and I remember Bert Kirk telling me with enthusiasm that Barnwell was a different place in those days. According to Bert, there were hostels for chaps and girls, all beautiful buildings, a billiard hall and a dance hall. He used to come home on Friday evenings specially to go to the dances. They had football team – The Barnwell Roosters!

Paddy Kitchen

Barnwell ford looking towards All Saints' church. On the left is Friar's Close.

CHAPTER 6
Shops and Shopkeepers

Bob Cheney, who took over the gents' and ladies' hairdressers and tobacconists on the corner of West Street and New Street, Oundle on 1 March 1936, retired on 15 August 1977.

On the Corner

Our shop was on the corner of West Street and New Street in Oundle. When my father, Bob Cheney, who was a hairdresser, took over the business there was a ladies hairdresser and then in the middle was a shop that sold tobacco and pipes and on the other side was gent's hairdressing. During the war we employed people to do the hair and then when he came out of the army he started to do it, but he didn't like it so he shut that part of the business and enlarged the shop and that is when they started to sell fancy goods.

Ann Cheney

Founded in Warmington

Our family business was founded in 1882 at Warmington in what is now known as Woodlawn House in Church Street. It was called Craiglea House then. It was started by the eldest of five brothers, and my father's uncle. The eldest and the youngest of the five brothers worked together as smallholders, pig breeders and butchers. The eldest brother died when he was thirty-one and the youngest one, Walter, took over the business. He ran it for a great many years and then in 1911 he bought the business of John Bull who had a butcher's shop in the market place in Oundle. That was when the Brudenell's came to Oundle.

Philip Brudenell

Helping in the Grocer's Shop

I was born in Thrapston, right in the centre. I was born over one of the grocer's shop my father ran. It was Tomlinson's Stores and my father's name was Mr Palmer but he kept the original name. He ran the store up until about 1966 and then he retired. We sold everything including paraffin. Goods came in large containers and we had to weigh everything out on a Saturday afternoon. We weighed things into four ounces, half a pound, a pound and two pounds. The sugar was always two pounds and it was always put into blue bags.

Some things we put into paper twisted bags that we made up ourselves. I know with sweets, we put them into little pieces of paper that we twisted at the bottom and folded over at the top. We poured golden syrup into tins people brought, though heaven knows how we did that! Vinegar was put into customer's

bottles. Sugar was in blocks and was cut into pieces with sugar cutters; salt would come in 28lb blocks and soap was the same.

It took a long time getting things ready. We used to take orders the week before and deliver them the next week. Mother used to collect orders on her bicycle and dad used to deliver in the van. We delivered to Brigstock, Keyston, Denton, Raunds, Addington, Aldwinkle, Stoke Doyle. He was often out until nine or ten at night.

One Christmas, somebody wanted some crystallised pineapple. We had crystallised everything – all sorts of fruits you can imagine except pineapple. So my dad sent me up to Grants in London to buy some. I was about thirteen at the time and I took the train. It cost me four and sixpence return.

Joyce Bird

The Coffee Tavern

My brother Ralph bought The Coffee Tavern and he sold the other shop down the lane. It used to be called Avondale before that and there was a dentist above it. I think the dentist was called Mr Pears. He sold it to Peter, our brother.

Audrey Knight

Tall Stools

We used to go from Great Addington to Kettering or Northampton to buy our clothes. There was a big store in Northampton called Adnitt Brothers. It was a fascinating place. You would go in and there would be rows of girls behind the counters all wearing black, shiny dresses. There were tall stools to sit on and the store would have shop walkers who wore morning coat. I can remember being lifted up as a child and put on one of the tall stools. It was easy to see what was going on then.

There was a little contraption that ran along and when you bought something your money was put into a little container and it whizzed along to the cashier. The cashier would take out the money, put in the change if there was some, and a receipt, and send it back to the counter.

Mary Thomson

Cleaning Fish

I remember a fish shop there more or less opposite the post office in Thrapston. I was coming up there one day and it had been raining quite heavily. The slab was open at the fish shop and the fish were on it and there was a great big puddle of water just outside. Well, this lorry hit the puddle and all the water went over the fish. So the old chap came out with a watering can and washed the fish down and nobody was any the wiser!

Eddie Rowe

Changing

You think that Oundle hasn't changed but it has. The buildings haven't changed but the shops have. My father wrote some notes he called 'The Changing Face of Oundle'. At one time there used to be five butchers when we first came here in 1936. There was North's (where Johnson's is now); Brudenell's, (where Trendell's is); there was

The London Central Meat Company which was next door to us along West Street; Jack Wade's was also along West Street, on the corner of Setchell's Yard and Frank Seaton's was in North Street just past Latham's Alms Houses.

Ann Cheney

Three Shops

My grandfather, Edwin Hooton, had three shops in Oundle – one shop he sold to the International Stores, he had another shop where Goldsmith's is now and in North Street he had the Temperance Hotel. All the parents of boys at Oundle School used to stay there. Mowbray's, the painters and decorators, bought it off granddad. He sold

The Anchor in St Osyth's Lane, Oundle, now a private house. Most of the houses were demolished to make way for the Co-op Extra supermarket.

Hayward's shop at No. 4 North Street, Oundle.

mainly groceries and used to go round to the villages on his bike.

My brother Ralph had the shop that is now a children's shop in St Osyth's Lane where he sold groceries. First of all, he had The Angel and he sold groceries from there. When he took it over, the tramps used to live in part of it.

Audrey Knight

Hayward's Shop

We had a shop in St Osyth's Lane where the children's shop is now. It was a family business and my father bought it in 1946 off Cecil Clark. We sold hardware, china and glass, and toys. We moved from St Osyth's Lane to North Street, next door to Owen & Hartley's where there is now a gift shop. Gwen and I lived above it.

We ran Hayward's Hire Service and hired out crockery, glass and cutlery and we are just closing it down. We had been doing this since 1947 and it has been going steadily ever since. We loaned things all over and at one time we could do over 150 covers.

Tony Hayward

The Smell of Coffee

There were several grocers' shops in Oundle. Amps was where Dillons is now. The thing I remember most about Amps was that they used to grind their own coffee. I think they did it in the basement because as you walked down the street there was this lovely smell of coffee rising to meet you! Percy Amps was there then.

There was Claridges, which was opposite the Roman Catholic Church where West End Stores used to be. On the opposite corner, where there are now houses, was Dixon's Corner Shop. The International Stores was where Oxfam is now, Moore's General Stores and The Co-op in West Street where Bateman's have their Art and Antiques now. Wyman's was another grocery and that was in New Road.

Ann Cheney

Wood

As I remember it, it was all wooden fittings inside Amps shop. There were wooden drawers and a counter that went all the way round the shop.

Jill Fletcher

Small Shops

There were quite a lot of small shops in Thrapston. Dillon's, or The One Stop Shop as they call it now, used to belong to Jack Green. He was a stocky man in build, about five foot eight with receding hair and always had a word for everyone. He used to open the

Tony and Gwen Hayward in the 1970s in the shop in North Street.

Mr Hewitt in his glass and china shop in West Street, Oundle, in 1976.

shop about half past five in the morning. In those days all the lorries used to come through Thrapston and they all used to pull up here. It was very busy.

Eddie Rowe

From Top to Toe

Redheads were bakers in West Street, Oundle. That shop is now the music shop. Next door to that was a wine shop. Dixons was also a baker and in the Market Place was Greens that became Flettons and is now the opticians. They delivered bread and so did Todds of Barnwell. They moved to Market Harborough. Then there was Warner's in West Street.

Cunnington's were greengrocers in West Street. Marlow's, opposite, just past Victoria Hall was like a private house and you went up some steps and turned to the left into the shop. Where Oundle Cobbler is was a greengrocer called Barber.

There were five gents' outfitters and tailors. Thomas More's was near Trendalls and was owned by the Laxton family. Maddisons was near Mary Hull's cake shop and they used to employ two tailors. One of those was John White's father. John Parker ran Wilkins and Rawthornes was in West Street and so was Bellairs, who did mainly repair work and according to my father, had a shop front like an illustration from Dickens.

Davidson's was a ladies shop and haberdashery in the 1930s. So was Townsends, that was on the corner of Market Place and North

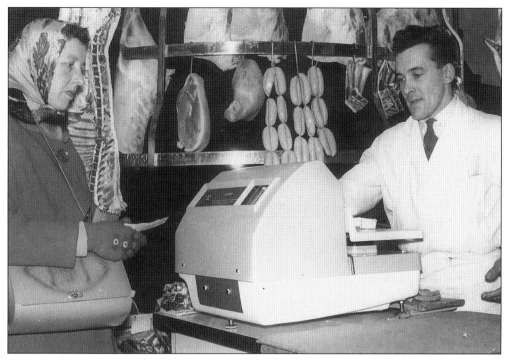

Philip Brudenell serving in the family butcher's shop in Oundle.

Street and there was Miss Lloyds at No. 4 North Street.

Cottons was, and still is, a shoe shop and there was Blacks in the Market Place who also sold shoes.

Ann Cheney

Family Butchers

My forebears, my great-uncles – and even my father – reckoned to be butchers; they wouldn't sell anything else. They were general butchers, in other words we didn't specialise as, say, pork butchers. We sold beef, lamb, pork and all the bits and pieces like the lards, the drippings, the faggots and the sausages. That was our business. In those days we didn't sell poultry. With rationing coming we

had sold what we had in two days!

Cleanliness was of great importance and I would think a day and a half every week was spent cleaning – swilling and scrubbing and polishing. There was a brass plate on the front of the shop that said 'Brudenell Family Butchers' and as a young lad I remember cleaning that twice a week. There were copper letters on a brass background and in the winter your finger as it went round the letters was like a piece of wood. It was frozen!

Philip Brudenell

Sit on the Steps and Wait

Howitt's, the Saddlers were in New Street where the Chinese restaurant is today. We used to go down some steps and be met with this wonderful smell of leather. Mr Howitt used to do the saddles and he made our school satchels. If you had a little hole in your satchel you would go and ask him to repair it. While he did it you would sit on the steps and wait.

Jill Fletcher

Rails to Roll the Barrels

Smith's Brewery was at the end of North Street in Oundle. In Blackpot Lane there were rails running down the road where they used to roll the barrels.

Ann Cheney

Everything but Newspapers

We closed our shop in the High Street in 1998. My parents went to that particular building in Thrapston in 1919 just after my father came out of the army. Originally we were on the opposite side of the road, next door to Barclays bank. My uncle was running the business then because it was just a branch of a bigger business in Kettering. It was called W E & J Goss, my grandfather and great-uncle. The shop where I lived was at No. 34 High Street. We sold toys and books, wool, stationary and cards. We kept sewing threads and needles, all useful things. Mother was asked if she would do newspapers during the war but she didn't want to. When the war started my father said it was not doing much for the war effort just to be running a shop, so he went to work at the Thrapston Washed

Howitt the saddler in New Street, Oundle.

Sand & Ballast Company in Bridge Street and mother took over the shop.

When Barbers the greengrocers, which was the next shop to ours, was being altered, they took down their side of the panelling and found that the wall between our two shops was a heap of rubble on the floor. The whole building appeared to be held up by a pier of bricks and one wooden post in our shop that was rotting at the bottom!

Pru Goss

A General Store

In my dad's day there used to be two cottages where Goddard's is, and one was a shop. It was lived in by Mrs Ogilvy and she sold general things.

Norah Blunt

John and Elsie Goss who came to Thrapston in 1919 and opened a shop that became well known in the town.

Starting in the Gutter

Oxfam was in a shop at the corner of Jericho, which is now Stu Pots, and it was rented from Mrs Lane at Ashton. We were the keyholders and when our business was closing I asked a lot of questions and eventually threw my lot in with Oxfam. That was in the 1970s.

It was very much part time because we didn't open until ten in the morning. When I first joined I remember one item that was made in a little village in Tibet. It was a multi-coloured bag that was very pretty and I think sold for about £1. They sold and sold. We were give a fortnight's notice to leave the shop so we found an empty chapel opposite the Chinese takeaway at the other end of town and we stored things there and we stood at the market on Thursdays. Then we

were offered the shop where the old fire station used to be and from there to where the Onkar Indian Restaurant is today.

Frances Pearce from Southwick was the first person to introduce Oxfam to Oundle. She and another lady started with a chair and a suitcase in the gutter in the market place on a Thursday. They went from there to the market building and it was run from Cambridge.

Gwen Hayward

So Many Grocery Stores

The post office in Elton used to sell groceries and Mrs Weatherington had another grocer's that was just below the post office. Mrs

The opening of the Oxfam shop in Oundle. From left to right: Frances Pearce, David Wills, Julia Byrne (retail manager), Guy Stringer (director of Oxfam), Gwen Hayward (shop leader) and Jenny Caborn (volunteer and window dresser).

Oakley had a grocer's shop where the hairdresser's is on the bottom green. There were two bakers – Mr Reedman and Mr Butler. Mr Reedman's was opposite The Crown and Mr Butler's was on the main road next to the garage. There was a butcher's shop on the bottom green next to the grocer's shop. The blacksmith's was on the main road, just on the corner near the village hall. Mr Oakley was the blacksmith but when he retired, Mr Wicks took it over. There was a shoemender by The Crown called Mr Hitchcock.

I used to take our Sunday dinner to Mr Reedman, the baker in Elton. I think we had to pay but I can't remember how much.

Dorothy Osborne

Islip's Sweet Shop

Mr Crawley kept a sweet shop and general store in Islip. He sold everything. He used to say to me, 'Good morning! And how are you today?'

Phyllis Whittaker

Mr Gray's Shop

There was a driveway at the end of the nine arches on the left hand side in Thrapston and there was a shop there with motorbikes in that belonged to Mr Gray. He was the father of Mr Gray who is at Gray's Garage on the Oundle Road. Where Nine Arches is was where

Loakes and Petits the builders was. Then there was a row of houses and there was the dentist, Mr Pears. At the end of the houses was another little roadway and that was Scott's Joinery.

John Jeffs

Tools to Lend

We had an orange cutter that we used to lend to people and an bean cutter. In those days we preserved the beans in salt. There would be a layer of beans and then a layer of salt. Then we could have runner beans at Christmas. We used to pickle eggs in buckets.

Joyce Bird

Almost Anything

Lenie Brown kept a shop in Wollaston along the High Street. You could buy almost anything in her shop.

Frank Palmer was a cripple. He had a three-wheeler invalid chair with a steering wheel and one leg was always stuck out in front as he went along. He was a tailor in Wollaston.

Jean Woodward

Whatever You Needed

When I was a youngster you could set up house in Thrapston. There were shops that sold everything. On the corner there was butcher Johnson's, Herbert Johnson's. If you followed the path round you came to The Plaza, the picture place. If you went down a bit further you came to some double doors and if you went through them, that was the council property where they kept their equipment – carts and whatever.

On the other side of the road, opposite the Plaza, you came to the back of Harry Wilson's property. He used to keep paraffin in tanks in his sheds and he used to deliver it all round the villages in a little van. He had a tank in the van with a cap on and you went out to fill your tin with two gallons for your paraffin heaters. We are going back now to the 1930s.

On the left hand side of the main street in Thrapston coming from Islip, there was Saxby's butcher's shop all decorated out in white, and the front of Harry Wilson's where he sold accumulators, wirelesses and bicycles. Next door to him was Olive Sharp who sold papers, sweets and ice cream. The Swan Hotel was next to Olive Sharpe's and it had

Staff of Tomlinson's Stores, Thrapston in 1949. From left to right, back row: Mr E.M. Palmer, Mr E. Morson. Front row: Miss J. Cooper, Mr H. Mundin.

a big area for putting horses and carriages. Next to The Swan was a hairdresser' shop and I think there was a little jeweller's before you came to Mr Stubbs the fishmonger's.

Harris's sold wirelesses, accumulators and sweets and ice cream. Next to Harris's was a passage and then there was The King's Head and next to that was a grocery store that I think was called Indochina. They had shops in many towns including Kettering.

John Jeffs

Always in Brown

The White Hart Hotel was on the corner of Chancery Lane. The opposite side was a little house and shop that was next to Barclays Bank. I can't tell you the name of the lady in the shop but she was always in brown, always in brown. I think she sold ladies' clothing.

John Jeffs

The Butcher Moved

When the estate at Barnwell was sold by Mr Czarnikow, it was split up and Mr Payne didn't buy his butcher's shop which was where the new houses were built just above me, but moved to the other shop next to No. 8 Barnwell.

Eileen Woolman

Village Shops

There were three shops at one time in Titchmarsh. There was the post office and shop, there was a general store at the far end

of the village towards the church and then down the hill going out of the village there was another shop on the left. They sold drapery and the newspapers on Fridays. This shop was owned by Mr Twelvetree.

There was one bakers and two bake houses in Titchmarsh. The one at the bottom used to bake the bread and on Saturdays people used to take cakes to be baked. On Sundays it was Sunday lunch they took. The bake house at the top of the village was originally thatched and you could take your Sunday lunch there too. At Christmas, we would take the Christmas cake to the bake house and my aunt, who came to live with us after my mother died, use to say, 'You must tell Mr Abbot not to let it sink in the middle!' My aunt was Mrs Annie Knight and she came to live with us bringing her husband, two children – Les and Eileen – and a foster child, Arthur O'Dell but we called him Billy Knight. That meant there were seven of us living here.

Raymond Gray

Over 130 Years in Business

The business was started in 1871 in North Street, Oundle by my grandfather, Robert Charles Cotton and we are still trading under R.C. Cotton and Sons. The shop frontage is still there. It was a butcher's shop until recently and is half way down on the right hand side. From there the shop moved to where Johnson's the butchers is now and moved to these premises at No. 7 Market Place in 1900. My father was born in 1900 and grandfather died in 1932 so my father, Philip and his brother Hector, took on the business. I remember the shop being much darker than it is now. As one came in there was a large, glass display counter in front of the entrance and to the left was a counter with a long mahogany top that had to be polished regularly. The floors were wooden that father used to sweep and periodically oil.

It is bigger now because we incorporate what was the living room and the kitchen and we use the upstairs rooms as storage. It was about two-thirds of the present size and at the back there was a screen that made a separate department. We sold shoes and probably quite a lot of agricultural footwear. In my grandfather's day they were making boots and shoes to order, with the majority produced in factories and brought over to the shop. At the back was a repairing area and prior to that, it was where shoes were made. My grandparents lived behind and above the shop but I can only remember my grandmother living here. She was rather a fierce looking lady with grey hair that used to be auburn. She was a typical Victorian with long skirts and dark clothing. Before we went into her living room we had to remove our shoes. There were romantic Victorian pictures on the walls, a kitchen table and a kettle always boiling for a welcome cup of tea for anyone who came in. If she saw what we stored in there now, in one way she would be disappointed but in another quite pleased that the business is still continuing.

After she died, father's elder brother, Uncle Hec, lived in these premises and when he retired, I came back to help and over the years we moved things around, redecorated and gradually extended and expanded.

Stuart Cotton

A Much Better Town

We were outfitters and sold boots and shoes,

Robert Charles Cotton who started the family business.

principally for men but we did sell some dresses. The shoes were bought from fairly local manufacturers like Loakes and Barretts and Holdfast. The clothes came generally from Mumbys of Newark or D.G. Gurteen of Haverhill in Suffolk.

My grandfather started as an apprentice with a tailor and outfitter in Exeter and then he decided to branch out on his own at a time when, I think it was, The London North Western Railway was building across the valleys to get the mining traffic.

They chose Thrapston because it was considered in those days a much better town than Oundle. It was on the junction of two main roads, it had a market – which Oundle didn't have in those days – more shops and two railway stations.

Philip Loaring

Whartons and Hordens

In Wellingborough there were two big shops. On the left hand side of Sheep Street there was Whartons and on the right there was Hordens. You always went to Whartons for your books, Christmas presents and Sunday School prizes. Hordens was a toy shop. Just round the corner, which is now all pedestrianized, it used to be two-way traffic and there is a shop called Green and Valentines which was the local draper. That is where we had to get our school uniforms. So many of the little shops – grocers, jewellers – have all disappeared from Wellingborough. When the Arndale Centre was built they demolished a lot of lanes where there were lots of tiny shops and cottages.

Jean Woodward

Three Fishmongers

There were three fishmongers in West Street. 'Fisho' Stokes was nearly opposite and then there was Shuts, which was further down and Ganderton's was at the end.

Ann Cheney

Barnwell People

Before Mr Todd was the baker in Barnwell it was Mr Russell. Mr Fred Russell and Mr George Russell were brothers but it was Mr George Russell who had the bakery. Mr Fred Russell was in the First World War and when he came back I think he was the postman.

Mrs Pask had a shop in Barnwell. When we were young we always called her Annie Kisby. She married Mr Pask. I think she brought up a nephew and we always called him Den Kisby and he married Dolly Cole. He was her first husband. We used to go and buy sweets there and she used to make her own sweet bags from a couple of squares of paper she rolled up to make a little bag. We bought mostly boiled sweets. We were given a ha'penny to buy sweets.

Eileen Woolman

Putty Allen

Where Sylvia Allen lived in Barnwell, just before Dora Robinson's old house, was a shop. Putty Allen, who was Sylvia's father, used to keep a bike shop there and sell bikes and everything under the sun. I bought my first bike off him. It cost me seven and sixpence in old money.

Norah Blunt

Elegant

Clarke's the watchmakers used to have a shop where Norman's is now and Mr Addison was a bespoke tailor who had a shop in the Market Place where the baker's shop is now. He used to keep the Old Hind public house which was in West Street which he looked after at night. He was a very elegant man. He was tall with a wife about half his size.

Reg Sutton

Neville Ganderton (right) outside his fish, poultry and game shop in Oundle.

Fish and Chips

Ganderton's had a big open window and all the fish was displayed on a sloping counter. You could get fish and chips from there.

Jill Fletcher

A Long Market

The market stalls were all along the main road in Thrapston on both sides. Outside Barclay's Bank they used to peter out but they used to start just below the Natwest Bank where the chemist is. They were on the road and the stallholders stood on the road and customers walked along the pavements. The traffic was not there then. Market Day was always on Tuesdays. There were petrol pumps outside on the forecourt at Heighton's Garage, which was just up from Barclays

Bank. I am certain there used to be a trough there which was filled with water so the horses and cattle could have a drink.

The Corn Exchange was next door and I remember there used to be dances there on Saturday nights. Lynn's was the ironmongers. Years ago I think they sold funeral furnishings such as coffin handles.

Next to the yard of The King's Arms was Arthur G Brown the auctioneer and further up was The Fox pub and that had an archway where you took your ponies and jigs through and tied them up at the back. I used to drink lemonade there when I was a boy.

John Jeffs

Everything For Sale!

In Thrapston there was Cawdell, a big shop that was almost like a London store where you could buy everything from pots and pans to furniture to clothes.

Philip Loaring

Haunted

Our shop was where the butcher's, Johnson, now is, and Trevor's the hairdresser was, at numbers 58 and 60. We moved to the shop when I was three years of age. The building was altered when we made the two shops into one but when we moved in the stairs weren't finished to get to the second floor and the bedrooms. We had a ladder right from the ground to the second floor where one of the windows was taken out. I remember my eldest brother, who was eleven years older than me, carrying me up to bed on his back up this ladder.

My father told us the shop was haunted

Petch were grocers in Thrapston.

because he didn't like us going down and mucking about. We used to love sneaking in and hiding behind a rail of coats and listening to him talking to customers. He said it was haunted by Marriott's ghost. Marriott's ghost had started to make a suit for someone and he finished the jacket but he didn't complete the trousers so his ghost came back to complete the trousers! There was a man called Marriott who owned the small shop.

Philip Loaring

The Electricity Shop

On the corner of Oundle Road was the electric light shop. I think, years ago, it was up Hortons Lane. It had big windows. Opposite was Cordells. That was three storeys high and they sold furniture on the bottom floor, bedding on the second floor and ladies' wear on the top floor. Next door was a sweet shop belonging to Mr Heffer. Along there were some houses and one was a barber's shop. There was Palmers, a grocery shop and where butcher Johnson's is now there was a pub, I think. Loarings were men's outfitters and next door they had a shoe shop . That is where butcher Johnson is now. You come to the front entrance to the cattle market and beside that is the Natwest Bank and then Cordell's the chemists. Going back in years, there was Benny Barber who sold fruit, vegetables and flowers.

Goss's is Tasty Bites now. They sold kiddies toys, knitting wool, polythene bags, needles, cotton, puzzles and all your writing stuff. It was a very handy, useful little shop. It never changed for sixty years.

John Jeffs

Corner shop on the corner of Benefield Road, Oundle, opposite the Roman Catholic church. It was once owned by Mrs Johnson who had an assistant called Mrs Dixon. Some years ago it was demolished and new houses are built on the site.

Pancake Day in Oundle, 1977. The photograph was taken outside Brudenell, a butcher in Oundle with the staff in party mood. From left to right: Richard Trotman, Angus Watson, Martin Trendall, Chris Jackson and Nigel Afford.

Personal Service

Mr Weatherington, who used to keep the shop in Middle Street, Elton, had a carrier's cart and he would go into Peterborough on market day and if you wanted anything he'd bring it back for you.

Dorothy Osborne

Where They Lived

The bakehouse was on the corner of the green and next door, at No. 3 Barnwell, was Mrs Russell's who lived there for years. The baker's name was Mr Todd and people used to take their Sunday dinner there to cook while they were at church. I can remember going from No. 31 with Miss Abbott, who lived at No. 30 and used to take me to church on a Sunday. She had a tin, covered with a white cloth, and she'd leave it at the bakehouse and collect it after. In those days the rector was Mr Dallimore.

Opposite, on the other side of the brook next to No.8 Barnwell, is a thatched cottage that Mrs Best lived in for years. Before that Lady Seton lived the other side of the Reading Room. The post office in my youth used to be up at The Stone Cottage where Mr and Mrs Akroyd used to live and Dolly Coles kept the shop that David Brown then bought. The shop belonged to Mrs Pask who married Walter who was something to do with the Manor. It was called the castle in those days and it's gone back to being called that now. Dolly Coles' first husband, Dennis Wells, was Mrs Pask's nephew.

Norah Blunt

Clerical Orders

There was another outfitter in Thrapston called Touch. His was the Church of England outfitters and my grandfather was the Baptist outfitter.

Philip Loaring

A Change

There has been a complete change in shopping in Oundle. We never had to go into the town to shop at all. We had only lived here two or three days when Percy Amps was up here in his car introducing himself. Then he would come on a Tuesday morning, take our order and by four o'clock in the afternoon it would be delivered here. It was the same with Philip Brudenell's father. They did the same and delivered the meat. Milk and bread was delivered by the co-op which was in West Street.

We went in on a Saturday to look around and meet people.

Reg Sutton

Changes

Oundle has had a lot of changes but it is still the same. The town centre itself has seen changing shops and businesses; there are less shops in West Street than there used to be. We have become a little semi-dormant but we couldn't provide work for everyone who lives here.

Philip Brudenell

CHAPTER 7
Leisure and Pleasure

Queue for the Victoria Hall Cinema, Oundle in 1957.

First in the Country

Oundle had the first municipal cinema in the country, which was opened in 1947 in the Victoria Hall and run by the council. The opening was announced on the radio in a programme called In Britain Now. The usherette was Miss Richards, a grey-haired lady, with a torch who would rush up and say, 'Are you boys behaving yourselves in the front there?'

There were three prices: 10d in the first three rows, 1s 9d in the middle and 2s 3d in the back three rows. There were three changes of film a week and two showings of each one. I think Alec Wright did some of the projection work.

Andrew Spurrell

Ruling the Hair Waves

We used to go to the cinema in the Victoria Hall. You could sit in seats that cost 2s 3d, 1s 9d or 10d. We mostly went in the 1s 9d. The 2s 3d had plush seats but the others were wooden seats. My father used to have an advert there: Rule Britannia, Britannia rules the waves, And so does R.W. Cheney!

Ann Cheney

Cushion

There were two rows at the back with plush seats, that must have been gleaned from another cinema, with tip-up seats. Otherwise you took a cushion with you. You got very good films very early on.

Gwen Hayward

Anne Brookfield as a Girl Guide.

Nothing You Can't Do!

The Young Farmers used to meet in the Girl Guide hut. The first time Joyce and I went I think there was one other lady there! We had rallies, stock judging, and you were graded and scored points on what you did. We had social evenings and played games like bingo, and team games such as passing the orange and sucking a pea up on the end of a straw and carrying it to the end of the line without dropping it. We had dances too. We were in the Brownies and the Guides before that. Miss McQueen from Wadenhoe ran those. We learnt everything we knew from her. She used to say, 'There's nothing you can't do. Other people might be able to do it better but there is nothing *you* can't do.'

Anne Beesley

Pole Floating

We played cricket and football but the countryside was so lovely in those days with woods. We would go pole floating in the brook just below here. We got pieces of wood about two feet long. Sometimes they got stuck in the bank and we couldn't release them. I remember we cut little bits of paper once up for a paper chase but we got in trouble from the farmer and we had to go and pick them all up. That was Mr Abbot. He had just pasture fields and no arable land. There were other farmers such as Mr Roland Wood, Mr Jellis and Mr Charles Hankins.

Raymond Gray

William Thomas Gray with his wife Annie and son Edgar. William Gray fought in the latter part of the Boer War in the Northamptonshire Militia.

Country Dancing

Harold and I first met in Oundle at The British School which was along a small road opposite the Catholic Church. It wasn't a very big place. I think it was at a whist drive. There were always a lot of whist drives in the villages. I had gone from Hemington and Harold had gone from Cotterstock. I met him and spoke to him but that was it! Then, Miss Wickham – she was really called Mary but people called her Molly – used to take people around in her car to do some country dancing. We met in Barnwell Reading Room. There were a lot of people who used to go – Barbara and Ian Hamilton, the Berridges, Mrs Crosby, Dora Robinson. They were mainly Barnwell people and it was great fun. Somebody played the piano, I think it was Jessie Roughton who is now Jessie Richmond.

We used to go dancing at the bigger houses too. We were invited to go to places like Dene Park and I seem to remember we went to Boughton House. We would dance and the people there would join in. If they didn't know what to do we would show them.

Miss Wickham used to drive us and on the way back she would drop me at Barnwell where I would pick up my bike and cycle back to Hemington.

Gladys Ashby

Plenty for a Boy to Do

We used to play cricket. There was Billy Mayes, Billy Culpin, Len Jeffries, Brian Jeffries, the Chamberlains, Lawrence Ray and Alec Ray. We played against Thorpe, Bythorn and Thurning and Barnwell. At Barnwell I remember there used to be a concrete wicket when we played. It was on the left as you went out to Thurning.

We found enough to do in Titchmarsh. As a boy we would roam around the fields. There was The London End and Polopit War. Polopit is another part of the village. As youngsters we used saucepan lids as shields and we used to pelt each other with stones. At one time in London End there were thirty people living here. Les Jeffs was one of the Polopit boys, as was Sonny Bright. We heard once that a lot of them had gone to Wicksteed Park so we went and rubbished one of tents in a hedge. We never mixed with the Polopit people in the school playground.

Raymond Gray

Tea at the School

We used to have a garland on May Day and two boys would carry it around the village on a pole. Miss Fancourt came, she was the schoolmistress, and she got Mr Crowson to build a maypole and we used to carry that round the village. Then we used to have a tea afterwards at the school.

Eileen Woolman

Vote for the Queen

As May Day approached we would have a ballot in school to choose the May Queen. There was a little coach that the boys pulled and it was decorated with flowers. We would go around the village carrying flags and we used to stop at Mr Abbot's farm for cake and lemonade. Then if it was fine we would have tea in the Rectory gardens.

The rector was Canon Luckock and he was here for fifty years. I believe his father was Dean of Lichfield.

Raymond Gray

Scouts

Tony started the scouts in Oundle. He had been scoutmaster in Kettering and he started the scouts with two or three others. After a lot of haggling they got a piece of land from the council and my brother in law, Bob Barton, found an ex-military hut and it was erected on the corner of New Road and St Peter's Road.

Gwen Hayward

Home-cooked

Titchmarsh Feast Day was on Whit Sunday. There was a special service in the church and it was always the custom then for all the people to have their relatives visit for tea when we always had ham. After I left school I worked for a time at Smith & Grace's at Thrapston and one old chap who used to paint the pulleys used to say, 'Have you got the ham ready, boy?' It was home cured ham.

Raymond Gray

The Servants' Ball

When Major Cooper was living at the Manor in Barnwell, he always had a ser-vants' ball every year and the servants always invited a friend. My brother,

May Day in Titchmarsh.

Harold, worked there at the time and I was always asked to go. They always took place at Christmastime.

Major Cooper had a tennis court built there so we could all play and we had a tennis club.

I remember when the old Princess Alice, Countess of Athlone, used to come and stay at the Manor. She always came to church.

Eileen Woolman

Sunday Stroll

On Sundays were used to go for a walk. That's what people did: they worked in factories all the week and on Sundays they would put their best clothes on and go for a walk.

Jean Woodward

A Busy Life

We went to the pictures twice a week. That was at The Plaza. We also went to Kettering by bus at the weekend. There was a bus from Thrapston to Kettering every twenty minutes and it used to cost 1s 3d. That was in the 1940s.

I was in the army cadets – that was two nights a week – and I was also in the Youth Service Corps. The Youth Service Corps was a sort of youth club with a 'patriotic mission'. We used to go round with a handcart collecting newspapers and aluminium cans for the war effort. We used to take them up to the council offices which were in the old Union Workhouse on Midland Road.

Philip Loaring

Inside the Plaza Cinema, Thrapston in 1967.

Regular Whist Drives

Dora Robinson had a lot to do with the country dancing in the Reading Room. At one time we used to have a regular whist drive there every October. Miss Parker ran an evening for the mission to China. I know that when the war started, everybody complained that we'd given all that money!

Norah Blunt

Many Uses

The Temperance Hall in Thrapston had the YWCA and they showed films there. During the war it was a canteen. Everything seemed to happen there. There were a lot of army convoys going through Thrapston. There was a camp at the top of Huntingdon road.

Pru Goss

Choral Society

There was always a choir at Elton which was started before my time. They formed a choral society in the village and the two amalgamated together. It was a Methodist choir and the choirmaster, Mr Reedman, formed it into a choral society. They used to meet in the school, I think it was on a Tuesday. We used to go to the Oundle Musical Competitions before it was called the Oundle Music Festival.

Dorothy Osborne

Elton Choral Society at the beginning of the 1930s.

Bowling

We used to go to the Bowling Club in Market Road and to dances in Kettering and at Wicksteed Park. There were about twelve of us and we used to get a mini bus to take us for a night out. There wasn't a lot to do in Thrapston. At the Corn Exchange there used to be dances before the auctioneers took it over.

Eddie Rowe

Dancing in Alma Street

I had a friend called Barbara Potts who went to the High School and her mother and father used to run the youth club in Wellingborough in Alma Street. I would go with her on a Saturday night and we used to do old time dancing. We did the barn dance and the Gay Gordons and I think we may have done The Lancers. It was a social evening. Some times we went to Grendon Hall for a tennis weekend.

Jean Woodward

A Long Walk

We used to go to Peterborough for the pictures. There were lots of picture places there – The City, The Broadway, The Palace. We used to go to The City because it was nearest to the bus stop. If you missed the bus you had to walk – and I've done that a few times!

Dorothy Osborne

The Place to Go

There used to be dances, plays, wedding

receptions, dinners – everything like that went on in the Corn Exchange. There used to be concert parties there and I remember one of them included Bill Waddington who played Percy Sugden in *Coronation Street*. We lost a lot when we lost the Corn Exchange.

Pru Goss

To Market

My father would go to the market nearest to Christmas and bring a tree home. I can remember going to do our Christmas shopping in Kettering. We would go in the buggy with my parents and we would go into the grocer's shop where there would be wonderful smells. There would be everything there and you could do all the shopping in one place.

For Christmas lunch we would have goose and vegetables from the garden. My mother would make a sage and onion stuffing and we would have apple sauce. There was Christmas pudding and mince pies and there were always nuts and raisins and dates.

Mary Thomson

Carol Singing

We used to go in little groups to sing carols all round the village at Christmas. There was a grocer's shop on the top road there, where the pine antique shop is now. It used to sell everything and we would go there to spend our carol-singing money and buy Christmas presents.

The choir used to sing carols in the front hall at Elton Hall in Mr Granville's time. Lady Margaret used to have a big meal for us afterwards. That stopped when the war started.

Dorothy Osborne

Thrapston Amateur Dramatic Society in a production at the Corn Exchange in 1930.

Oundle Gilbert & Sullivan Society's back room workers. From left to right: Ernie Cox, Sid Falvey, Jim Graham.

Night Out

If we wanted a night out we would go to Peterborough. Close to the Cathedral there was a YWCA and we would stay overnight there. We didn't go very far.

Gladys Ashby

Words and Music

The Oundle Gilbert and Sullivan Society started sometime in the late 1950s and I joined in 1968. I couldn't do the performances unless I could get a week off work and when I started in the practice we had two weeks holiday a year. There were three of us and I have always been the youngest. I have always done the surgery. I get terribly cold and I hate the winters but in those early days we never had proper clothing. Nowadays you can keep yourself really warm when you go out.

I had brucellosis which I picked up from a herd. I went into hospital for four weeks but it took me about six months to get my strength back. Other than that I can't think I had more than four days off in thirty-nine years and not a single day off in the last ten years.

When I was in the army during my National Service, I was out in Hong Kong and we used to play a lot of the Gilbert and Sullivan records so I knew them pretty well. I played a bridesmaid in *Trial by Jury* when I first went to the Grammar School in 1950. When I first joined the Oundle G&S, the musical director was Henry Thurlow who kept the Rose and Crown, and his wife, Dorothy, was the producer. I played the part of Richard Dauntless in *Ruddigore*. For the next thirty-one years I had a major part in all but four of them.

We formed the Oundle Singers, two and a half years ago with Shirley Burchell, Diana Audrey, Hilary Gore Robertson, Cynthia Davies, the two Jackson boys – Michael and Barry, Colin Pendrill and myself.

I also did eleven years with the Stamford Shakespeare Company at Tolethorpe. I was a character actor with them. I had some wonderful parts – Bottom, Sir Andrew Aguecheek, Touchstone, Polonious, Laertes. When they first went to Tolethorpe Jim Clancy of C & G Concrete helped us with money but after a few years we got a mortgage and bought him out. I was one of the original guarantors.

Andrew Spurrell

A Lively Time

The travelling fairs used to come on both the greens at Elton and there was usually quite a to-do. People used to get drunk, as I understand it, but I was too young to know about that. They used to make the rides go round by winding a big handle. It was like a hurdy-gurdy. There were roundabouts and swing boats, as I remember.

Dorothy Osborne

Smelly Brook!

We used to have country dancing in the reading room at Barnwell. At night we had to keep the windows shut because the brook smelt so terrible.

Harold Ashby

Moving Round

There wasn't a Great Addington Feast Day but we used to go to Heigham Ferrars Feast. I think it was held in the field just outside. We would always go to Peterborough Show but there was also a county show. It used to move around; it was at Rushden, Wellingborough or Kettering.

It was very interesting because there used to be important people who used to open them. At Peterborough, I saw Prince Edward – who became Edward VIII. He was a funny little man who kept fidgeting. He was terribly nervy.

Lord Burghley, the athlete, and his lovely dark haired wife who was the sister of Princess Alice, Duchess of Gloucester, came to open the county show once.

Mary Thomson

Bus There, Taxi Back

We used to catch a bus from Thrapston, mostly on a Sunday night, to go to the pictures in Kettering. It used to leave Kettering to bring us back at 10.20 and if the picture ran over and you wanted to see the end, you had to get a taxi home. We used to get a lot of taxis!

Eddie Rowe

Money for an Outing

I don't know exactly when it was but suddenly they decided to have Rose Day in Barnwell and give this one rose to Princess Alice as rent for the school. Up until then we always had a May Day.

When I was May Queen we used to go to school in the morning all dressed up. The boys

Princess Alice, Duchess of Gloucester, bowling for the pig, at a fête on the rectory lawn in Barnwell in 1956. Percy Marriott looks on.

used to have poles with flowers on and the girls used to carry bunches of flowers. We went all round the village, singing and dancing. There was a maypole in the school playground and we danced round it to music from a wind-up gramophone. As it ran down it got slower and slower so we danced slower and slower. Then it was wound up again and we'd speed up again. We used to collect money and that paid for us to go for an outing.

Then we would all go down to the Manor for tea in the servants' hall. We had cake and doughnuts and jam sandwiches. For two years, and I don't quite know why because it would be when I was at Barnwell school, we were all invited down for strawberry tea. I shall never forget it because all we sat around trestle tables on the terrace and there were huge, great bowls of strawberries, bowls of sugar, bowls of cream, lumps of plain cake and little bits of bread and butter if you wanted it. That was when Colin Cooper kept the Manor.

Then they let May Day drop. Every village round here has May Day except Barnwell! When Coopers lived in the Manor we used to have a big fête there on Whit Monday. People used to all come down from London for it.

Norah Blunt

Old Time Dancing

We went to dances in Brigstock and Kettering – the Central Hall in Montagu Street. We didn't care for the modern dancing so we went to the old time dances. There were Waltzes, the Valeta, the Barn Dance, the Military Two Step and the St Bernard's Waltz.

Florence Gray

Dancing

We used to go dancing in Highgate Hall. In those days it was ballroom dancing and we did the Valeta, the Waltz, the Quickstep, the Barn Dance, the Foxtrot, St Bernard's Waltz, the Military Two step and the Palais Glide. We used to have whist drives in the village hall, too.

Dorothy Osborne

Home Made

My first little car was made in Thrapston. It was a Clyno and was made along the road that goes to Denford. It was grey with grey upholstery.

Florence Gray

Come to the Fair

There was what was known as The Wagon and Horses field where the fairs and circuses were held. The Wagon and Horses was a public house on the corner of West Street and Mill Road (where 'Pud' Rice used to live). Between there and South Road is Southbridge Close which was built on The Wagon and Horses field. The fair used to come to the town twice a year. There were coconut shies, rifle ranges and dodgems.

Philip Brudenell

Easy to Get Around

There were many buses that used to go through Thrapston in the 1950s. It was quite easy to get around in those days. There were two stations – the Midland and the Great Eastern, I think it was. On the Midland we used to be able to get to Oxford. We used to go to Hunstanton on a Sunday. The train was always full. We used to be able to get to Hunstanton for 4s in old money. We would get there for half past eleven and then there was the Sunday opening of the pubs from twelve to two. You could get a lunch and a pint if you wanted it. Then we used to come back about quarter to six in the evening. Once every six weeks they ran a train to Yarmouth. That would cost 4s 6d.

Eddie Rowe

Bank Holiday Fete

The British Legion fête was always held behind Lime House on East Road on August Bank Holiday Monday.

Philip Brudenell

Regular Cricket

There always used to be a cricket match between a Sandringham Eleven and Barnwell every year.

Norah Blunt

Meeting Place

When I was growing up I joined the Young Farmers. We used to meet in Oundle and it was a very active young farmers club in those days. I was a very shy lad and found it difficult to go out and mix with people but with the Young Farmers it was an excellent opportunity to meet people. We met at The Talbot. One of the earliest speakers we had I remember was Freddie Smith, the vet in Oundle. He operated on a crop-bound hen on a table in The Tabret room. The smell was awful! I was treasurer, then I became chairman then I became secretary.

I went to a young farmers' dance at Glinton and there wasn't much going on there so I came back to the centre of Peterborough and there was a dance at the Town Hall. Just inside the door were two young ladies and nobody seemed to be talking a great deal of notice of them, so I asked one of them to dance. That was Ann. I asked her what she did for a living and she said she worked in a bank. She lived in Alderman's Drive, in Peterborough and they had cycled to the Town Hall. I asked if I could see her home, but I couldn't leave the other girl, and so I put both bikes in the back of the pick-up truck. That was how I met my wife. The other girl married my good friend, Jim Singlehurst, from Benefield.

John Preston

Two Tents

There used to be two marquees in the Hall grounds for the horticultural show. One was for the exhibits and one was for the teas.

Dorothy Osborne

The back of Lime House, Oundle, home of the Spurrell family in 1956.

Tennis Club

We had a tennis club up at the castle. There was a court inside the old castle and then there was another tennis court at the back that was originally built for the staff. There weren't enough staff so we had a village tennis club and we had a pavilion up there. Then the Duke of Gloucester built a ruddy, great garage on it!

Norah Blunt

Princess Alice, Duchess of Gloucester, with the winners of the tug o' war at Castle Farm, Barnwell. From left to right: Princess Alice, policeman Alan Richardson, Ted Waite, Gerry Allen, Cyril Kelly, the rector of Barnwell, the Revd Peter Bustin and Graham Young. A young James Rutterford looks on. The event was part of the 1977 Silver Jubilee Celebrations.

A day's rabbit shooting in Woodford.

CHAPTER 8
Wartime

John Simpson of Warmington in the Home Guard.

Covering All the Villages

My father, Henry Simpson, was Company Commander of 'A' Company in the Home Guard. It covered all the villages as far as Easton-on-the-Hill. All villages became sections and a sergeant was in charge. Tansor had Sergeant Beech. If there were thirty people in the Home Guard in a village, as King's Cliffe had, they became a platoon. Anyone who was in a reserved occupation during the war was eligible to join the Home Guard. You had to do some-

thing, whether it was the ARP or something else to do with the war effort. I joined under age. I can remember that my father, because of his position in the Home Guard, was sent various things to store safely. One of the first things I can remember, before they issued rifles, we were sent corrugated tubes, about six feet long. The government welded bayonets on the end, called pikes. Then all the Home Guard were issued with those. Then rifles came and then uniforms.

John Simpson

Staff at Elton Hall when it was used as a convalescent home during the Second World War.

A Convalescent Home

During the war Elton Hall was first a girls' school and then it became a convalescent home for servicemen.

Dorothy Osborne

A Land Girl

I was in the Women's Land Army at Hemington. I was on Ben Measures farm for four years. I had to do all general farm work. It was fun then; one machine now will do a whole field of corn but it took us about a week to 'stook' a field. We used to have a bit of fun as we did it, throwing things at one another. I lived in Hemington and used to come backwards and forwards to see Harold here in Cotterstock. I lived in a cottage there with one other land girl. They pulled that little cottage down.

It was an arable farm but they had some cows and some pigs. Guy Measures was killed in the war and Dick wasn't a fit man. I think he was in London when we first went there but he came back home and he ran the farm with his father. I loved to take a couple of horses across the fields to the blacksmith's at Great Gidding to have them shod! The blacksmith was called Yeomans and there was a man called Len who worked for him. That was the highlight of my day!

I didn't like carrying the chaff from the thresher. It was very, very dusty and dirty and you had to take turns to carry it in a bag over your shoulder to the barn.

Gladys Ashby

The Shop Closed

In the Second World War, the Warmington shop was closed because there was no staff –

they were called up. Similarly, the Oundle shop had a staff of about six and four of those were called up in 1939. At the end of the war, my great-uncle Walter decided it was time he should retire and he offered the business to my father, Edgar Brudenell. My father had worked there for various periods between the wars but his main job at that time was opening new shops for Dewhursts butchers. The first one was in Cambridge, the next in Letchworth and he opened two or three in Northampton. He came back to the family business to join his uncle in 1935 but left again and went to open Norths in Bridge Street next to Woolworths in Peterborough. We lived in Peterborough but in 1944 we moved back to Oundle and I have lived in the same house since then.

Philip Brudenell

Knitting

We used to knit socks, mufflers and balaclavas for the army. We also collected rose hips to make rose hip syrup.

Joyce Bird

Invalided Out

I left school in 1934 and I worked at Smith & Grace in Thrapston until January 1937. They made big pulleys on shafts and there would be some on electric motors. I worked in the machine shop office. I wanted to go in the air force and I had to do some swotting because we were not taught algebra and all that in our school. They were taking people in then from fifteen and a half to seventeen and a quarter.

That was before the war. I managed to scrape in. There were 1,250 in that entry that year. When I went in I was ten days off my seventeenth birthday. I was sent to RAF Halton. I was only in the Air Force for five and a half months because I had pleurisy and then tuberculosis. I came home after spending two months in the RAF hospital and I was sent to Rushden Sanitorium and I spent eight months there.

Raymond Gray

Congratulated

There was a searchlight near Tansor Grange dryer. The actual diesel engine had to be 500 or 600 yards away from the searchlight because of the noise. The soldiers had a camp near the dryer and I spent a lot of time with them, playing darts and snooker. These soldiers used to go every night to The Anchor pub, which was bang opposite the main gate of the church in Warmington. On one particular night, I was the only one on duty when the telephone went and it was the commanding officer from Peterborough who shouted, 'Put the bloody light up!' and rang off! I turned the handle of the telephone, which rang to the man who looked after the engine. As luck would have it, my brother David answered and he got the engine going. When the indicator came up to power, I got the light up and put it on Warmington church. When they saw the light on the church, the soldiers knew they had to rush back – fast.

That was the night that Coventry was raided. The next morning, we were congratulated for getting the light on so quickly!

John Simpson

Elton Red Cross during the Second World War.

Bombs

There were incendary bombs that landed in Titchmarsh in 1940 and they burned two cottages down at the top of the village. The night before, it was very busy with aircraft. On Wednesday evenings we used to go for a walk round the roads to Thrapston. We had just got up to where the Rose and Crown used to be and there was a terrific crash and a terrific bang. I thought they had bombed Islip furnaces but it was somewhere near Sudborough. We went on and when we got to the Oundle road there was another flash and another bang so we turned back. The next morning I go up the street and the houses are smouldering and the furniture is outside. Apparently, they dropped at first in Mr Wood's stack yard in Chapel Street.and he sent for the fire brigade but then he cancelled them because he wasn't aware there were houses burning up the street.

Raymond Gray

Spam with Apple Sauce

During the war we ate Spam which was fried and we put apple sauce on it. There were rations. There used to be bacon in a piece and it was literally all fat except there was a streak of lean going through it. That was very good and you could do various things with that. You could cook it for dinner with vegetables or for breakfast with tomatoes and toast. And you could eat it cold.

Phyllis Whittaker

Evacuees

During the war, evacuees stayed with different people in the town. You had to have them if you had room. Mrs Hassall was in charge and she would come and count your bedrooms. We had two attic rooms in our house in High Street and we had a lady and her daughter stay with us. I had three little teddy bears I was very fond of and when they left I let the little girl choose one to take with her.

Pru Goss

Chicken Pox

We had one evacuee for one day because she came with chicken pox but we had people staying with us all through the war. They were mostly people who were relatives or friends of relatives.

Joyce Bird

Fire Watching from the Bus Shelter

I was only young during the war but I volunteered to go fire watching. I think we spent a lot of time in the bus shelter! You had to make squares on your windows with strips of gummed paper that were about an inch and a half wide. There was blackout material for curtains. Some people had the material on frames that they fixed in the window. You couldn't have any light showing at night. We had paraffin lamps them and I remember our mother turning the wick down every time you went out or there was a knock at the door. We had a thick door curtain.

Dorothy Osborne

Disappointment!

I was a messenger with the ARP. I never had to go on any messages!

Raymond Gray

Answering an Advertisement

Right at the beginning of the war there was an advertisement in *The Daily Telegraph* asking for people who had an expertise in a language to report to London. I answered it and was taken on by the Field Security Police. I was trained for a month in South Wales where I joined the 'Ack Ack' and had my military training and when that was completed I was sent to what has now become the Intelligence Corps in Winchester. I was there until the beginning of 1941 when SOE, that had just been created, needed someone who spoke fluent Spanish. They recruited me and I was sent to the New Forest where there were 200 Spaniards who were ex-Republicans who had joined the Foreign Legion and been sent by the French to fight at Narvik. When Narvik fell and France fell, they volunteered to come to England where they could be useful saboteurs if Spain came into the war.

I lived with them for about a year, then I was told to go up to the Orkneys. I was told to get the midnight train going north and on the train I would be contacted by a representative of MI5 who was going to find out whether Spanish vessel that had been taken in by the navy was in fact under German control. I was a stooge and I helped him in the interrogation. I then went back to the SOE group in the New Forest, and a week later I was told to join MI5, where I became an interrogator. I was responsible for interrogat-

David Simpson of Warmington.

ing all Spanish-speaking people who came to the country during the war.

Alec Payne

Trainer Station

At Sibson airfield there was a trainer station. One of the planes came down just near the chapel and it was just as if the chapel was on fire.

Dorothy Osborne

Central Distribution

We had our own slaughterhouses in Warmington and in Oundle but at the start of the war they closed all the slaughterhouses because there was central distribution by the Ministry. The only slaughtering that was done through the war was the farmer's pigs as each farmer was allowed to have one pig killed once a year. Sometimes there was a casualty sheep.

Philip Brudenell

Saving the Horses

At Hemington House there was a big Dutch barn that was one of the biggest of its kind at the time and this day we had to go on top of the stack inside. There was a tractor next to the elevator and the exhaust of the tractor was too close to the stack. I was going up the ladder at the time and my land army smock was on top of the ladder. I saw the flame going up towards it. There was such a commotion that followed. The barn was all burnt down but the fire didn't go to the house.

We had to take the horses out of the stables that were next to it towards the village. We walked them up the road away from the farm and we stood with these five horses for a long time before it was safe to take them back.

Gladys Ashby

Christmas in the Washhouse

The man who looked after the engine for the spotlight lived in our washhouse at Tansor Grange Farm all through the war. He made it beautiful; we spent Christmas in there with him one year!

John Simpson

Guarding Barnwell

I was in the Home Guard and I spent one night in the stables up at the Rectory where we used to have our head quarters. We had our radio and telephone and we were there with Tom Litchfield. It was awful: the mice were running about.

They used to go and man the water tower on the Hemington Road. There was a sort of radio station along Oundle Road opposite White Lodge and this was manned by the air force from Wittering. That's where I met Sandy Morrison who became my first husband.

In the field on the opposite side of the road was the army camp. The concrete place was originally built as an ordinance depot.

There were prisoners of war living in Barnwell and working in the fields. We had two staying with us at home. Rudi was the first one. He was Italian and he was a marvellous carpenter and made some doll's furniture for my sister's baby. When the Italians went back we had two Germans.

Norah Blunt

Taking Readings

Near Tansor Grange we had a bombing range and it covered nine or ten fields. There was a big, very big target made from corrugated tin. Many a time I have seen Blenheims and the American super-fortresses on bombing practice. They used smoke bombs. There was an RAF hut on top of the hill near Tansor Wold and another near the entrance of Tansor Grange. When a bomb dropped, smoke went up and the men in the huts took readings from different angles.

John Simpson

Tom and Elizabeth Osborne during the First World War.

A Cup of Tea Out

We used to go to the gents' hairdresser in Oundle to have our hair cut. It was behind Owen and Hartley's. We biked to Barnwell station and we would try and hitch-hike into Oundle from there. I remember going and having a perm at Thrapston.

Wherever we went, we would always have a cup of tea out before we started back. There was a place, up some steps, that was opposite the hairdressers.

There was a little bus that left from Oundle station and called at all the little villages until it got to Kettering. We used to go just to look at the shops. We once walked all the way from Kettering to Titchmarsh where

Tom Pearson in the Home Guard at Wollaston.

As far as my memory serves to the last war, if there were six or seven in a family, they would buy something like brisket or breast of mutton which were the cheaper cuts and they could make the meat go further. The ration was done not in the weight of meat but the price of it. You had 10d worth or 1/- worth. If you had a shilling's worth of fillet steak you'd get a matchbox!

Philip Brudenell

Biking to the Station

We used to leave our bikes with Mr Elcock at Barnwell station. They were ever so good to us land army girls and let us leave anything there.

Gladys Ashby

we were staying at a hostel before I went to Measures. It was twelve miles. We thought we were bound to get a bus or a train but there was nothing so we walked the whole way.

Titchmarsh hostel was next to the church and the vicar, Canon Lucock used to pay our wages and keep an eye on us. There were some little thatched cottages opposite the hostel and the people there used to invite us for tea sometimes. We had cream buns and cucumber sandwiches.

Gladys Ashby

Brisket

I have a price list from the First World War that will go to Oundle Museum eventually.

Filling

We had a lot of suet puddings during the war because they were very filling when food was quite scarce. We would have apple puddings and treacle puddings. We were lucky because we had access to fruit and my father, Tom Pearson, grew vegetables. There was a lot of bartering. We were luckier than people who lived in a town. We always ate things in season.

Jean Woodward

Walking Everywhere

When we first came to Hemington we had no bikes and we walked everywhere. One of the girls had worked at a departmental store in Liverpool and we ordered two bikes from there. The post office man, Stan Wriggles, brought them to us from Barnwell station. All we got was two wheels and a frame! The farm men – you called them farm labourers then – fixed us up with baskets on the front, a pump and a bell. Dick Measures had to have a bike because he couldn't use his car. If there was anything on, especially if it was at Oundle School, he would take us. Some big musical was on there and I always remember, he biked there with us.

Gladys Ashby

On Duty

In the Home Guard, a platoon was made up from men from Fotheringhay and Southwick. Two of them had to be on duty every night on top of Fotheringhay church.

John Simpson

Always Fill the Kettle

During the wartime, at night you always filled your kettle with water before you went to bed because you never knew if there would be any in the morning.

Reg Sutton

Ammunition

We became very sophisticated in our weapons and we had a lot of ammunition. They made me Ammunition Officer for 'A' Company. We had three or four tons of high

explosives so they built large huts in a lot of villages – Easton-on-the-Hill, Duddington, King's Cliffe. They gave me a brand new motor bike and it was my job to look after it and issue it out. I had to see that it was kept in proper conditions.

In those days I spent more time in the Home Guard than I did on the farm. I went on an eight-week course with the army learning about looking after the ammunition. That was in Bury St Edmunds, I think. Before that I went on a six weeks course down at Dorking with the Commandos where I learnt about small arms. I did very well and got over 94% in the exams.

Every weekend, 'A' Company met and fifty or sixty men stayed at Lilford Park under canvas where they learned how to use rifles, machine guns, Bren guns and all modern

Madelene Brookfield as a messenger with the ARP in Thrapston.

equipment. After these courses and the exams I was one of the lecturers.

John Simpson

Under the Desk for an Hour

I was five when the war began and once, two fields away from the school at Tansor, there was a plane crash. The teacher thought it was a German plane and had us lying underneath the desks for an hour! We always had to carry a gas mask with us.

Anne Brookfield and American serviceman, Jack O'Neil, who married her sister Madelene. Jack was at the Ideal Clothing Factory in Thrapston, which was taken over by the American's as a supply depot.

There were some barracks at Tansor. They commandeered Tansor Court during the war and that was a training ground for soldiers. Where John Gould keeps his sugar beet was a parade ground.

John Preston

Mickey Mouse

We didn't go without much and anyway, we were so young we didn't notice. We had gas masks, with Mickey Mouse faces but as children we didn't know any better and we knew we had to take them round with us.

When we went to Brownies there were no street lights and you came home with a torch, which wasn't very bright. We used to see pictures of bananas. I remember going to Cunnington's and on their door there was a picture of some bananas. We didn't know what they were but when we had our first one we thought they were lovely.

Ann Cheney

Muddy walk

I remember Winnie Fleet and I got off the train at Barnwell one night and started walking towards Hemington. Instead of going right we kept to the left and went down by the Manor and up the Armston Road. We got to Armston and it didn't seem quite right. We must have walked on towards Lutton, through Polebrook and on to Hemington. We were very muddy.

Gladys Ashby

A Big 'A'

I was in the ARP. I lived in the village then and I painted a big 'A' on the wall. When there was an air raid on and somebody had to come out on a motorbike and knock me up. I'd go down to Perio, now Bierton's farm, and pick up Eric Cotton. We got our tin hats on and our gas masks and go on the motorbike to Oundle. Some times we stopped there all night. We sometimes had exercises at Corby simulating air raids.

Harold Ashby

Lie in the Ditch

During the war the golf course was bombed at Oundle when it was mistaken for Corby and there were three bullets down West Street. In those days it was only a nine-hole golf course. Not a great deal happened here although I remember a doodlebug going over the house. If we heard an air-raid siren when we were out walking as kids, we would lie in the ditch until the all-clear was sounded. There was no fear at all. If there was an air raid in the middle of the night we quite liked it because we would get a cup of tea at three o'clock in the morning.

Andrew Spurrell

Queues

During the war, people would find out from the station when we were getting a delivery of cigarettes and before they were delivered to our shop, there used to be a queue. In those days everybody smoked because you didn't know cigarettes damaged your health. We had to ration the number we let people have.

Mother ran the business while my father was in the army and when he came back after the war, she continued in the business until he retired and they worked together.

Ann Cheney

She Showed Him!

There was once a post mortem on some chap found dead in a barn. Dr Preston said put your cigarettes out! Eric Cotton had just had an operation for appendicitis and wanted to know where the appendix was. Dr Preston pulled it out and showed him!

Harold Ashby

Taking the Bus

I remember VE Day when there were great celebrations and parties in the streets. On that day, one of the double decker buses was parked in the market place waiting to go to Peterborough. One of the Oundle schoolboys came out of Bramston House and called all his friends to go for a ride. He climbed into the cab and drove off with a whole lot of Oundle boys on board! I don't know whether they got to Peterborough!

Philip Brudenell

Stuffed Marrow

During the war we would eat stewed rabbit or marrow that was stuffed with mince. My mother used to make something out of nothing.

Ann Cheney

US Hospital

At the base at Polebrook there was Jimmy Stewart and Clark Gable. They all came on VE Day with their army lorries and they used to drive us around. There were parties and a bonfire on the rec. Lilford Hall was an American Hospital.

Andrew Spurrell

Emergency Coupons

When rationing started in 1940, because we had a lot of village deliverers, we would get our registrations in and the number we had determined how much meat we would get. Each family would register with one butcher. If they went away then they would have to apply for emergency coupons. The Food Office in Oundle was in New Street, where Hunt & Combes is now. If you were going away you would take your ration book there and they would stamp the coupons of the appropriate week on the ration book and replace them with emergency coupons. They could be spent where you liked.

At that time there were ourselves and Norths who were the main butchers in Oundle. We had nearly all the villages – eighteen – on the northern side of Oundle for deliveries and Norths had those on the southern side. After we ceased deliveries that was a big change for the business. There was no charge for deliveries and it was when the SET – Selective Employment tax – started. That was around 1960 and was a tax on service industry. It did a lot of damage. If you were in manufacturing or exporting you could get it back, but businesses like ours could not. I decided then that we would no longer do deliveries which was about a third of the business but I was not earning money from it. We then doubled the size of the shop and people had a wider choice.

Philip Brudenell

Councillors in Oundle watching the arrival troops on a recruiting tour.

CHAPTER 9
Winters

Marjorie Spurrell (née Cheney) taking part in an ambitious skating demonstration.

Seeping Through the Bricks

We had open fires and coal was delivered in bags every week and put in the coal house. Our wood came from Elton Estates and was delivered once a week. We had stone hot water bottles to heat the beds. I've known mum take a shelf out of the oven and wrap it up and put it in the bed to warm it.

Winters were much worse than they are now. When we lived in Chapel Lane our house used to get flooded most winters. The Navigation Board, which is what the Water Board was known as in those days, used to come and tell us they were expecting the floods and they even used to help us take the carpets up. I have known the water to come up to the second step on the stairs. It never used to come in through the door, it used to come up through the bricks especially the ones in front of the fire place. We had a fireplace upstairs – I think most places had in those days – and our mother used to light a fire in the bedroom and we'd stay up there for two or three days. We had time off school and we used to love it because we could paddle about in the water!

Dorothy Osborne

Getting Together

They got a group of people together in Cotterstock and called them The Snow Clearing Group. That group kept together for quite some time.

Gladys Ashby

Snowed In

Gladys had been on a course in Bury St Edmunds and she came back and I met her in Peterborough. We bought a few pots and pans and we came back to the house here in Cotterstock which was partly furnished to spend the night. It was a rough old night. We were going to go to mum's for meals but we couldn't get up the drive. The snow was level with the top of the hedge so we had to walk up the middle of the field where it wasn't so deep. It was about ten days before anybody could get through to the village. That was 5 March 1947.

After the snow was cleared away it was very cold and the wind got up. Mother was down here and it was so rough, the plate on the cooker was jumping up and down. There was a temporary shelter over Chancel Wood and asbestos sheets were flying by the window.

Oundle schoolboys came and dug a way through so we could get out of the village.

Harold Ashby

Frosty Inside

When there was the bad winter in 1947 it was pretty dire. We had no gas in the house until 1949 and we had to use candles. We had a gas cooker and a gas mantle but we had no lighting upstairs except a gas mantle in my mother's bedroom and she had a small grate in there. We always woke up to see the frost on the inside of the window. We had an outside loo.

In 1963 I was married and living in Doddington but that was a bad winter because we were virtually snowed in for three days. It was difficult for the milkman to get through and walking was hard because the snow was so deep.

Jean Woodward

Snowed Up

On several occasions I had to walk to Islip Furnaces in the winter. That was about four miles. Coming home, a bus stopped and I got in and asked how much and he said don't bother. I got to Thrapston and started walking again. I got to the bottom of Oundle Road when you go up to the Titchmarsh turn when a gentleman stopped in a car. He told me he had to dig himself out twice on the way. The next day we were snowed in. The baker eventually got in. He came from Islip with a basket of bread over the fields. The parish council had a person detailed to organize things so they fetched us all out to dig out the top end of the village.

Raymond Gray

Delivering by Punt

The river used to flood regularly. That stopped all milling because the water was over the mill wheel and that happened most winters. You would get timber coming down the river, especially from the railway, and that damaged the wheel. I was always having to get new paddles.

When the weather was bad we delivered milk by punt. We had a punt that was about twenty feet long and very wide – it was an ex-river authority punt – and we used to pull it with a carthorse. If there was snow or you couldn't get over Nassington bridge because of flood water, we'd use the punt.

When we got to the station we would ferry people across the flood water to the railway.

Jack Starsmore

Lines Down

During the bad winter of 1963, I was responsible for the whole of the telephone network covering Oundle, Kingscliffe, Elton, Winwick, Cotterstock and Benefield. At night time, if there was an emergency and the exchange packed up, I had to go and see to it. In that year, the overhead lines, which went all the way to Peterborough, were brought down. One night, all the lines had come down across the Warmington road. You couldn't get along the Glapthorn Road and we had no water.

Reg Sutton

Ice Hockey

The river used to freeze over quite often in the winter. We used to play ice hockey or go skating and even, sometimes take our bicycles on the ice. That was fantastic because you used to have all sorts of crashes and people would disappear through the ice and have to be rescued! The water was only about two

feet deep so there wasn't any great danger.

The biggest fun we had was in the rec, which is now known as the Peace Memorial Park. Its original name was Kiln Close so it was where the lime kilns were. It had a very steep slope so we used to find tin trays that had been thrown out on one of the rubbish dumps and we used to toboggan down the slope.

Philip Loaring

Frozen Pump

We had our own pump for water but it used to freeze up in bad weather so we had to wrap it up. If it froze we had to pour a kettle of hot water over it. There used to be a lot of wells here but they have all been filled up.

Everywhere used to be cold in winter. We knew it would be perishing cold. We had an open fire and an old range. We had hot water bottles in the beds but I used to have a stone ginger beer bottle. If you kicked it out of bed at night it made a great bang.

Raymond Gray

A Wild Night

There were floods between Islip and Lowick in 1947. It was a bad year for that. I had a friend in Islip and she lived at the other end of the village. It was her birthday one Sunday and I went to her party. A gale got up, but her cottage was sheltered by trees from the force of the wind. At half past nine there was a knock at the door and my brother, Bertram had come to fetch me because slates were blowing off the houses in the village. It was a really wild night. He had brought a galvanised bath – one we used for washing the clothes in – to cover my head as I walked back with him through the village. That was 16 March 1947.

Phyllis Whittaker

Frozen Tortoise

In 1963, one of my tortoises had dug itself into the ground but not too deeply and it was frozen, solid into the ground for six weeks. When it finally got out about Easter time, it was cold but it walked out as if nothing had happened. The snow in 1963 started on Boxing Day and it was nearly as bad as the 1946-1947 winter. They soon got the main roads clear but most people in villages only went into town once a week so there always had food stores at home.

Reg Sutton

A Struggle to Manage

It was a struggle to manage in the bad winters before there were mechanical means for removing snow. In the '47 winter the snow on the main road was two feet deep. I walked to Laxton School that first morning and when I got there, there were only 17 boys out of 170. We spent the morning clearing the paths round the churchyard. When I came home and told father what I had been doing he said I could do that round the farm. All the pumps had to be thawed every day. For some, out in the fields, you'd take an armful of straw with you and tie that round them.

In '63 the underground water pipe froze. We struggled for three weeks to get water from one source or another and then I went to Peterborough to an electricians and asked if they had any means of applying electricity to a galvanised water pipe. They say yes, they could do it if we dug the holes in the ground. We dug two holes using picks and shovels and they put an electric cable around the pipe and within minutes the water started to trickle through.

John Preston

Near Lower Farm in Barnwell.